I0490070

ACKNOWLEDGMENTS

This book is not possible without the countless hours and energy spent by not only the people dedicated to get the book on the shelves but those who shared their stories of financial hardship with me. Your stories drove me to want to tell this story. I see and feel the pain you are in when feeling the burden of financial struggle. My hope is this book will help you climb out of the place you find yourself and teach others how to avoid the challenges you currently face.

CONTENTS

JR Haynie

DEATH
by
TWENTY

Managing Your Money One Small Decision At A Time

JR HAYNIE

ISBN: 9798392459643

Imprint: Independently published

DEDICATION

This book is dedicated to my incredible family. Lauren, without your constant support, this book would not be possible. To my kids, Oliver, Madison, and Julia. You all bring joy into my life each day.

CHAPTER 1

INTRODUCTION

"The man who never has money enough to pay his debts has too much of something else."
~James Lendall Basford

You can lose everything spending $20 at the store. Seems crazy, right?!! IT IS CRAZY, but it happens to so many every day. Today, businesses are great at creating marketing or pulling at your emotions to separate you from your money or what I often refer to as your "spend ability". More on that to come later... So, what does this mean? You go into a store planning on spending $10 and leave having spent $50. Can you relate? Multiply this event three or four times in a day and your budget is blown and you are left with very limited to no money in savings. The fact is, we get into real debt trouble to the point of bankruptcy if the behavior is not corrected quickly. The good news is with a little forethought and willpower you can avoid the pitfalls and avoid "Death by $20".

I began this idea when I noticed individuals of all ages struggle financially. At first, I didn't understand, so I dug a bit deeper. I recognized two profound truths.

1. Individuals don't go bankrupt because of large extravagant purchases.
2. Small purchases matter.

Small purchases make up the most of purchases we make each day. Heading to the store for $25 here and $30 there. It begins to add up by the end of the day. When we add other items that were unplanned into our purchase because we say "I'll just get it because we're already here" we can cause big problems later. Death by $20 may seem dark and cloudy at first but with a new spending mindset, life can become more liberating. Saving on one small purchase at a time takes your dwindling savings account and creates a snowball of wealth.

A famous business investor and CEO of Berkshire Hathaway Warren Buffett was once asked why others don't follow his investing strategy. He answered, "Because people don't want to get rich slowly." Death by $20 shares the mindset that wealth is something gained over time and not an instant object gained overnight. Other books want to teach you how to "get rich quick" and often over promise and under deliver. Death by $20 aims to show you simple financial principles so when your facing purchasing decisions, you will make the best decision for your short-term and long-term financial well-being.

The goal of any financial help should always be to either increase the amount of money coming in or reduce the amount going out. Increase savings or decrease debt. As simple as it is in theory, the act of following a plan is challenging. When we breakdown the expenses we have each month, there might not be much remaining. According to a May 2019 Charles Schwab survey "Modern Wealth Survey" 59% of American families live paycheck to paycheck. It should be no surprise because the same survey said Americans pay more attention to how their friends spending habits than saving habits. [i] Implying we care about keeping up with our family and friends' appearances more so than the financial health of their financial portfolio. Often, appearances do not adequately represent financial health and wealth.

Let's look at a family making $65,000 per year or $3,500 per month after taxes and other deductions. Basic living expenses per month. Location can make a big difference in these numbers so adjust according to your location and expenses.

- Rent / mortgage ($1500)
- internet ($50)
- gas & electric bill ($120)
- water bill ($40)
- car fuel ($80)
- groceries ($350)
- school supplies ($45)
- loan payment ($250)
- tv ($95)

After the basic expenses, not much remains for new clothes, car repairs, medical bills, movie theaters, going out to eat, or anything else. The expenses listed above total $2230. This leaves $770 to spend on the non-essential "fun" things in life like dinners out or that new jacket you've been wanting for the past few weeks. If we divide the $770 by 30 days in the month, we get about $25 per day in extra "spend ability". This means, if we spend more than $25 per day on anything else, we have spent more money than we received and end up in the "Debt Breakdown" Image A leading to more debt and less money in the long term. When we spend less than $25 each day on average, we end up in the "Savings Breakdown" Image A. This is the sweet spot and if done for a long enough time, we grow our wealth and become financially free.

Image A

DEBT BREAKDOWN
Income
DEBT
Spending

SAVING BREAKDOWN
Income
Spending
Savings

Que the balloons and confetti!

It's as simple as this… spend less than you bring in. It doesn't matter the stage of life or the amount of money you bring in. $10 thousand or 10 million a year in income does not change the principles of this book. Of the many I've interviewed about their bankruptcy experience this simple principle was lost. I believe we understand the spend less principle when we look at big purchases like cars, homes, maybe even trips, or certain clothes that are high dollar value. High dollar value items have a shock value to them and are easy to notice when we are spending too much and often come with blocks built into the system to prevent us from making purchases too expensive through bank loan requirements. I've seen many lose sight of this principle when it's about a $5, $10, or $20 purchases. There are no blocks to these purchases. We are enticed and encouraged by wording used in marketing like "sale", "one-time only", or "value".

Nobody regulates the amount you spend on these items but yourself and we repeatedly make unplanned and unnecessary purchases in these price ranges. The unplanned $20 purchases begin to add up pushing us further and further into the "debt breakdown" from Image A. Death by $20 is just this, going bankrupt because we don't control the small purchases in our life. Rarely do we go bankrupt over large purchases mainly due to the blocks built into the process of obtaining the large purchases. We can literally lose everything because we don't control the small purchases. Not one purchase, but the culmination of many unplanned purchases over a (sometimes small) period of time.

The second meaning of Death by $20 is often, the habits developed in a persons' twenties will determine the financial freedom that person will experience later in life. The habits built in the twenties multiple the effect (good or bad) when the salary becomes bigger and the financial responsibilities of home ownership, marriage, children, and many more become a larger part of life.

So small purchases do matter and creating good habits early pays multiplied benefits later in life. Simple, right?

Lessons Learned in Introduction

- When you spend MORE than you bring in, you create DEBT.
- When you spend LESS than you bring in, you create SAVINGS.
- Small purchases do make a difference in your ability to save.
- Creating good spending habits early in adulthood pays multiple benefits later.

Notes

CHAPTER 2

BUILDING A FINANCIAL MENTALITY

"Start where you are. Use what you have. Do what you can."
~Arthur Ashe

We live in a truly remarkable age. We see incredible growth with innovation every day. New apps and new businesses delivering goods and services faster and more conveniently than ever before. If we desire a good or service, it's not hard to find it and we usually don't have to talk to anyone or go anywhere to get it. Just download the app and put in our information. It's that easy. Almost everything we want at our fingertips, but all too often our homes are filled with knick-knacks and junk holding no significance to our life. Subscriptions with monthly charges eating away at our wealth. At this exact moment, can you list all the services you use for TV, school, shopping, eating, transportation, clothing, social connection? In 2018, the Waterstone Management Group[ii] surveyed 2,500 Americans asking them to guess their monthly expenses on subscriptions[iii]. People guessed

$79.74 a month. When prompted by a list of services such as Netflix, Spotify, Birth box, Fitbit, Disney+, etc., they raised their estimate to $111.61 (a 40% increase). They raised their estimate a third time to over $237/month (a 197% increase) when shown additional services like WIFI, cellular service, and additional apps. Although entertainment and other expenses are a necessity of life, without check, those things hold you back from achieving financial goals.

We need to make purchases to survive both physically and mentally. The year 2020 proved in a dramatic, if not traumatic way, the need for physical and mental health, all of which costs money, time, and resources. The universe knows I enjoy a good fast-food run and a quiet evening watching my favorite series on Netflix. We make purchases almost every day of our lives and feel the cost when rent is due, the bill comes at a restaurant, or purchase tickets to the concert of our favorite artist. Purchasing items of need or want is exciting and brings joy into our lives, but if left unchecked or unplanned will leads to heavy financial burdens, bankruptcy, and challenging life decisions.

In 2018, the U.S. Census Bureau[iv] reported the average American family earned $63,179 per year. A few studies from 2010 – 2019 also describe the average income growing at a faster rate than the cost of living which means we can keep up with inflation and purchase more than the basic cost of living. This quickly transitioned in 2022 with the fastest rise of inflation in 50 years and is a great example of the transitions in life we need to be prepared for. Stories from recent generations of collecting tin for the war effort or gathering soda cans to trade for baseballs are fading from memory. This generations' ability to purchases goods and services with ease were the hopes of past generations. Less people die from hunger and disease. Less people struggle to provide a roof overhead. Affording a nice meal out is typically experienced more than once a week in many households regardless of race, gender, religion, and family upbringing. We find ourselves in a widening middle class, better equipped and better positioned for growth opportunities. Opportunities for financial saving and planning are also better than ever before through various private and public financial programs. Unfortunately, many in America and across the globe struggle to find the right balance between income and expenses. Basically put, they spend more than they earn, not because of basic living needs, but because of basic financial choices and find themselves drowning in debt. The only way out is through extreme financial measures like bankruptcy and liquidation.

As found in the Charles Schwab Modern Wealth Survey[v] in 2019, Gen Z, Millennials and younger generations are most likely to spend on experiences and products because of something they saw on social media. No one ever wants to be left out of the party or be seen as unable to provide the best for themselves. The social media illusion is often never achieved and a leading cause of the $6,124 average credit card debt per household per a 2019 NerdWallet statistics[vi]. (I was happy to see this statistic was down from 2016 when the average credit card debt was $16,000 per household. YAH!)

When compared to the average annual income of $63,000, the average credit card debt is 10%. For many this percentage is much higher and can many multiple times the amount of their annual pay. Until this is paid off, this means someone else OWNS 10%+ of your spend ability, plus on-going interest growth! Interest payments are no joke as the typical American household pays almost $1,200 in interest payments alone each year! This should make you angry! This should be seen as modern-day slavery! The difference is of course we put ourselves in this position! We will talk about good debt and bad debt, but we should all remember that if we have ANY debt, it means we have used someone else's money and until it's all paid back plus interest, they own a piece of our time and resources. Legal action can be taken if you don't repay the debt and you stand to lose much more than the original amount borrowed through added interest, stress, legal actions, and much more.

No matter your situation now, you can become free from debt. Your income level does not matter. Every day you can read of Hollywood stars who make millions of dollars a year and still declare bankruptcy. Sports athletes unfortunately often face financial ruin quickly after they leave the game. Professionally teams have even started to provide financial consulting to all players to educate them on proper financial management because it is a common issue. These principals act the same whether your income is only $20 thousand or $20 million.

Lessons Learned in Wealth and What it Means

- We underestimate the amount we spend on services and products.
- Expenses are essential to survive physically and mentally but should be monitored.
- Your financial freedom is impacted more by spending habits than by income level.
- Having debt means you used someone else's money and there is a cost for that.
- Debt means someone else owns your time or resources until paid back.

Notes

CHAPTER 3

THE PURPOSE OF MONEY

"The propensity to truck, barter and exchange one thing for another is common to all men, and to be found in no other race of animals."
~ Adam Smith

What better way to begin speaking about how to avoid financial ruin than by speaking about the purpose of money and how we need to view and understand the money in our wallet, purse, or bank account. Take a moment and think about how you use money…. You go to work and every few weeks get a paycheck. Most jobs in America will issue paychecks about every two weeks or maybe monthly. You've worked hard and finally the day has come where you get paid. PAYDAY!! This day is coveted among all other days. For some the day give relief to pay bills or cover a store run. Others, a day to go out with friends and enjoy the hard work you've put in. Maybe you've been waiting for payday to go try that new burger place that opened down the street or hit up that new bar around the corner from your place. If you are lucky, you don't live paycheck to paycheck. If you are living paycheck to paycheck, it's ok… you are not the only one. Many people do so for their entire lifetime. Life is easier if you are not living paycheck to paycheck, but today, money has become so fluid in a person's checking account, we hardly notice its presence before it is spent. Like my favorite dessert, it's gone before I blink.

It is easy to think that a person making more money doesn't have to worry about money or if the paycheck was larger, living paycheck to paycheck would be a thing of the past, but you would be WRONG! Living paycheck to paycheck has nothing…. I repeat… NOTHING to do with the quantity of money on a paycheck. Living paycheck to paycheck has EVERYTHING to do with how the paycheck, whether large or small is SPENT! We can't be naive to believe making more money is not better. Money affords us more things, but people making millions per year go bankrupt and large families of 8 or 9 make a modest income last for all their needs. They succeed or fail because of spending habits and an established financial mentality; not how much they earn. To really understand how we can better use our money, let's discuss what money represents.

Money has always existed but not in the way we have it today. In any community throughout history, trading existed long before dollar bills or coin currency. When I was younger, trading baseball cards happened in the playground at school. Trading with your best friend was probably the first experience you had dealing with "money" whether you realized it or not. Let's continue…

As a simple example, Let's say two farmers live near each other and one has a cow and the other has chickens. Both farmers want milk and eggs each morning for breakfast, however owning both a cow 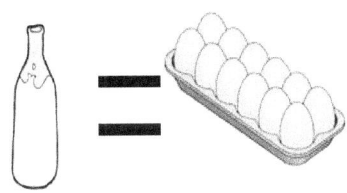 and a chicken is too expensive. The cow farmer also cannot drink all the milk he gets each day and is left with excess milk. The chicken farmer cannot eat all the eggs he collects each day and is left with excess eggs. So, what happens... the cow farmer takes some of the excess milk and trades with the chicken farmer for some of the excess eggs. Both farmers agree to the "price" of a can of milk and the "price" of a dozen eggs. They both agree one can of milk is equal to one dozen eggs. Both farmers benefit by the trade and now do not have to own both a cow and chicken to have milk and eggs. Trading allows both farmers to specialize and still eat a balanced breakfast. The cow farmer gets so good at raising cows and the chicken farmer gets so good at raising chickens, they have even more excess milk and eggs. With the additional excess, both farmers can now trade for other things like lumber from the lumberjack, metal work from the blacksmith, or flour from the wheat farmer. They can even trade milk or eggs for a service like going to the doctor or to see a lawyer.

Trading (or bartering) goes back to the beginning of human history. If I have something of value, I can use it to get something from someone else of equal value. In the farmer's story, they traded milk or eggs for similar valued goods which they needed. Pretty soon, the entire town has learned what is valued and trades accordingly, but there are difficulties with this type of trading. Eventually it becomes difficult to know what the dairy farmer values and to know what to bring the farmer to trade for a can of milk. For example, if you are a woodcraftsman and make beautiful rocking chairs, but the farmer already has enough rocking chairs for his entire family and visitors. He has no need for more so he values the additional rocking chair very little and would offer little to anything for you to bring him another rocking chair. Another challenge is when you only need half of a can of milk. You, as the woodcraftsman cannot bring the farmer half a rocking chair to exchange for half a can of milk.

Speaking in today's terms, if you are an engine builder and wanted to pay the doctor for a procedure you received, do you bring an entire motorcycle or only half of a motorcycle? How do you bring half a motorcycle? Are two halves of a motorcycle worth the same as a full motorcycle? I would bet if someone brought you two halves of a motorcycle and told you it is the same as a full working motorcycle, you would laugh them out of your living room and call them crazy. This is where currency notes come in handy. Currency allows you to break up that motorcycle into equally valuable parts. If a motorcycle costs $10,000. Half of that ($5,000) is worth the same as the second half ($5,000). You take the motorcycle value of $10,000 and break it up to by breakfast for your family, payoff a medical bill, and purchase that monster TV for the family room without having to guess what to trade. It makes trade faster and easier.

In America, "money" has transformed a few times to get to our current trade of the U.S. currency dollar bill.

1690 Colonial Note

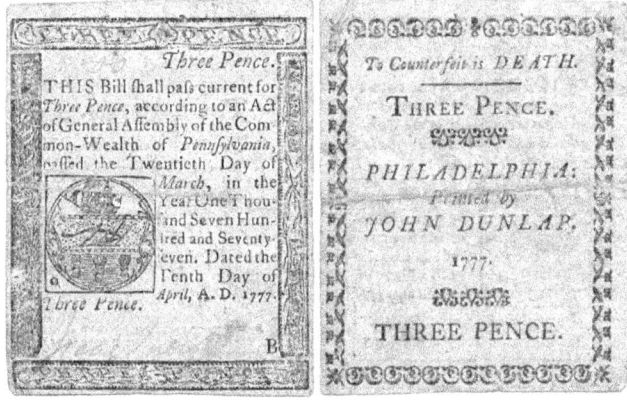

In 1690, Colonial Notes were a paper currency issued by the Massachusetts Bay Colony to fund military expeditions. Each colony used their own paper notes making it hard to travel between colonies. In 1739, Benjamin Franklin used his own printing firm to produce these colonial notes with added protection measures created against counterfeiting.

We notice counterfeiting is introduced to maintain the value and adoption is only to the point users believe the paper maintains the value in goods.

1775 Continental Currency

In 1775, the same year as the Declaration of Independence was signed, the Continental Congress issued Continental Currency to finance the Revolutionary War. This currency did not last long due to lack of backing by the 13 colonies and due to the rise of counterfeiting.

Counterfeiting again is a major concern and the financial backing is critical to the adoption of this new currency. Ultimately a failure but helped to launch the colonies into the war.

1861 "Greenbacks"

In 1861 and in response to fund the Civil War, the Department of the Treasurer issued currency with a nickname "greenback" due to their color. This has remained the color of American money ever since.

A pattern of issuing new currency to fund war efforts, with continued focus on financial backing to ensure adoption rates. If people don't trust the trade value, they prefer to go back to physical barter of goods for goods instead of goods for a piece of paper.

Most recent US currency

Through the next 100 years, small changes were added here and there such as adding presidential names to already printed portraits on the currency in 1889, adding the inscription of "In God We Trust" in 1957, to the most recent redesigns of the currency as we know it today beginning in 1996. Despite how currency has changed in design, the purpose has always remained the same. To create ease of trade and to provide a means of providing value to our economy. When the ability to trading is made easier, more trade occurs. This additional trading creates an economy boost and will increase jobs and create additional wealth for the city, state, and country.

Today, money has evolved so much that many spend what they don't have and have not earned. Going back to the cow farmer and the chicken farmer, this would be as if the cow farmer went to the chicken farmer and asked for eggs without providing any milk. The chicken farmer has three options at this point. (1) Tell the farmer no and to come back when he has some milk. (2) To gift the farmer the eggs with no expectation for repayment because the cow farmer has been such a great friend over the years. Or (3) to loan the farmer the eggs expecting repayment at a future date plus a little extra (interest).

In fact, the chicken farmer loans out a dozen eggs but instead of only receiving one can of milk, because they loaned a dozen eggs, the cow farmer is now required to pay one and half cans of milk to the chicken farmer to pay off the loan. We can quickly see how this can get out of hand if the farmer continually does this type of deal with many people in the community. Over the course of many deals, the cow farmer now needs to provide 300 cans of milk but only received the value of 200 cans of milk.

Unfortunately, when we see credit cards or numbers on a computer screen the banks provide us, we do not view our money in the same way as cash even though our "spend ability" IS the same! Money is a representation of the value we provide to the community. It is the value of the milk the cow farmer can provide or the value of the eggs the chicken farmer can provide to the community. If you take out too much in loans or don't repay your debts, your "value" in the eyes of the community diminishes and each time you want to trade you are required to give more interest for the same value. If the cow farmer does not payback the chicken farmer with one and a half cans of milk shortly, the chicken farmer will require him to pay two cans of milk the next time he wants a dozen eggs. Often, we view this as your credit score or your credit "worthiness". A low score means you are a bad cow farmer who never repays the chicken farmer. The purpose of money is to provide an ease of trade, but because so many institutions want to remove you from your money, if not careful, you can be left penniless and be seen as having no value. The opposite is also true. By remaining aware of your value, regardless of the amount of money you make each paycheck, you can increase your value and create wealth.

Lessons Learned in the Purpose of Money

- Trading (Bartering) existed well before currency.
- Paper currency exists to speed trade but relies on the trust of the population to maintain the value.
- Our value to the community is based on not only our ability to provide a good or service, but to also pay our debts.

Notes

CHAPTER 4

THE VALUE OF MONEY

"Price is what you pay. Value is what you get."
~ Warren Buffet

Many Americans don't think about a single U.S. dollar as having much value. Many fast-food establishments sell their cheapest, lowest quality items on their "dollar" menu for people looking for something quick and easy to eat. Not the tastiest menu items, but something to fix the hunger or to stop the oncoming "hangry" friend. One dollar cannot buy much in today's market and has thus lost the value it once held in our minds. It was not long ago when kids would go around the neighborhood collecting cans to turn in and receive 5₵ then spend the 5₵ on a soda. The entire soda cost 5₵!! It is hard to imagine, but if you ask older generations, they will tell you how everything was cheaper when they were a child. You can even notice today the price of everything has increased compared to a few years ago. Homes, cars, food, gasoline, clothes, everything increases in cost over time. There are numerous economic factors causing this increase that we will not discuss in this book but knowing the cost of things will always increase overtime is important to keep in mind. Where once we saw the "1-dollar menu" we are now seeing the "5-dollar combo" or the "20-dollar bundle". We must constantly ask ourselves what is the value of a dollar bill?

If you can, take out a one-dollar bill from your wallet or purse and lay it out in front of you. As you do so, ask yourself what value this one dollar holds. What can you buy with it? If the wind blew it away, would you chase after it? As you answer those questions, consider the scenario presented next.

If I asked a friend to give me one dollar, he would probably give me a strange look, but ultimately provide me with the dollar. Maybe he thinks I'm hungry and need a candy bar from a vending machine. If I went to him the next day and asked for the same thing, he might become curious, but still give me the dollar. If I continued to ask him for a dollar each day, he would eventually stop giving me the dollar.

Why?

What happened?
A dollar is not a lot of money, right?

Certainly, giving the dollar will not hurt him or put him in the poor house. The value of a single dollar did not change in his mind, but his actions changed because the value of each additional dollar changed. Asking for a dollar a day might not seem like a lot of money, but if I asked you for $365 on January 1st saying I would not ask for any more money throughout the entire year, you would begin to ask questions and consider the pain of giving me $365. Most people would think it's crazy for my friend to continue to give a dollar to me each day, but those same people, give the dollar away every day willingly and eagerly. They don't see how this behavior can lead to financial difficulty or worse, they <u>do</u> see it but give it away anyway.

Giving support to those in need is a great help to many and I'm not suggesting to never give your friend a dollar if they are in need, or that everyday purchases are not needed. What I see is many of us purchase without purpose. The lose vision of how much those multiple dollars can add up a create real financial value. We buy because we can, or we feel a purchase impulse while shopping. We purchase items not considered needed prior to entering the store. This adds multiple dollars to our purchases every day. We buy because we have money burning a hole in our pockets. We have the money so why not spend it…

In 2010, the job market was tough for college graduates as it was for anyone looking for a job. I found myself heading to Albuquerque, NM with no friends and no connections but with a new position as a fresh graduate ready to take on the corporate world. The only person in the entire state I had ever met was my new boss when I was interviewing for the position. I drove into town the night before my first day, signed an apartment agreement and headed to a local store to purchase an air mattress to sleep in a very empty apartment. I felt the pressure of my new position. I had been looking forward to this position and the sacrifices I had made for the past 4 years were about to pay off. I felt rich, but life was about to become expensive.

I will always remember my first paycheck. I was shocked! I had negotiated a good salary for my experience and when I broke it down, this would have been more money I have ever received in a paycheck. What I failed to see was the taxes, social security, Medicaid, health insurance, 401K disbursements, and all the things that are taken out of the paycheck before I even get a chance to spend it. Most people call this the "take home" amount because it's the amount of money you take home after all the deductions. The great thing about that moment was I learned how far my work effort went. I learned how much money I had to spend on things like food, rent, entertainment, and personal savings. I learned at that moment my "value of a dollar". How much of my effort does it take to earn one dollar? I remember at one point figuring out how long it took to earn one dollar. Then when considering a new item, I could tell myself how long it would take or how much work it takes to "trade" for that item. At the end of the day, money represents the time and effort we put in during our jobs. We trade time and effort for money which then trades for goods and services.

This is what I call your "value of a dollar". Knowing how much time and effort it takes to pay expenses, entertainment, and all the other items found in life. By fully realizing this value, you can adjust your spending accordingly. Ideally, knowing how far a paycheck will go to pay for a desired lifestyle should be calculated well in advance. Simply put, know your value and spending less than we bring in is the key to growing wealth. We work hard for our money, and we should be proud of the accomplishments our efforts achieve.

Knowing and understanding your "value of a dollar" can be a protection against others wanting to steal a piece of your value. Companies and everyone in the world want to separate you from your money. Less for you means more for me. Too frequently, others are willing to do whatever they can to take what you have earned and keep it for themselves. Don't let them take advantage of your hard work. They want to steal a piece of your financial value you've created. They do this through clever marketing and fake sales. Great effort is taken by businesses to encourage more spending and so you decrease your financial value.

Just as earning money should be purposeful, spending should also be done with purpose.

I married in my late twenties and had previously developed my own spending habits as a single guy. Getting married made me reconsider and readjust my personal "value" of a dollar. Life had changed and so had my thoughts on how money was to be spent. I'll admit my apartment was a typical bachelor pad and needed sprucing up. After we got married, my wife was up to the task and transformed what was a drab bachelor pad into a young married couple apartment. She went about making various purchases some for function and others for a new look and feel. OK, it needed a much larger transformation than I initially thought. Due to all these changes, her and I had to come up with a simple rule to avoid unnecessary spending. This rule has stuck with our marriage even as our income levels changed.

The Rule: "Do we have a place for it?"

> If (Name the item) had a logical use or a
> known physical place (and we could
> afford it), it would be purchased and used.
> If not, then it would be put back on the
> shelf.

I'm sure I became annoying asking that question, but this question soon became common in all our habits. If we don't think we need it when we are home, why do we think we need it when we are at the store? What is it about the store that makes items so much more enticing? Our spending habits changed after we got married. I ate better from her love of cooking compared with my mac and cheese and frozen pizza diet. With the change, we reevaluated our "value" of a dollar and made purchases with purpose.

In an article published on CBSNEWS in 2006 called Cutting through Advertising Clutter[vii] Walker-Smith was quoted saying "we are exposed to approximately 5,000 ads per day". It is probably even more being almost

15 years later. We constantly filter through these ads; mostly unknowing, and only focusing on the ads we find enticing. If we are only interested in 0.2% of all the advertisements, we see each day, we are enticed to buy or participate in something 10 times per day. 10 times every day we consider purchasing something from an ad created to separate you from your money. If the average cost of each item considered is $15, that will mean we could possibly buy $150 each day outside of the regular cost of living with rent and bills. Understanding your value of a dollar helps mitigate much of the noise these ads create in our mind.

 The worth of a dollar changes every day either through a personal life change or through the passing of time. We too must constantly evaluate the value we place on our dollars. We work hard for our money, and we must protect the value we have created, because if we don't, nobody else will.

<u>Lessons Learned in the Value of Money</u>

- Don't buy it unless you can identify the exact use of it. (Does it create value?)
- Reducing the ad noise is important to avoid unnecessary spending.
- Know your financial value you bring home each day and keep spending below the line.

<u>Notes</u>

CHAPTER 5

FINANCIAL ABSTRACTION

"It's all fun, until you get the bill."
~ Common Saying

Abstraction is defined as "the quality of dealing with ideas rather than event" and can roughly be translated as something which exists only as an idea. Financial Abstraction is a piece of a financial trade which exists only as an idea (not physical).

In 2017 the United States Federal Reserve did a study called "The Federal Reserve Payments Study: 2017 Annual Supplement" [viii] The study showed card payments grew from 103.5 billion with a value of $5.65 trillion in 2015 to 111.1 billion with a value of $5.98 trillion in 2016. Simply showing the use of cards for making purchases is more common today than yesterday. This trend will continue to rise because the easier it is to make a transaction at store, the more money you will spend. This is why stores invest in checkout-less grocery stores, smartwatch, and tap-and-pay payment options. The more a company makes us feel separated from the loss of the trade, the more likely we are to make additional purchases.

When was the last time you made a trade when making a purchase? You may think you traded money at the store the other day when you made your last purchase, but if you made the purchase with a credit or debit card, you didn't trade anything. You walked in, picked out a few items, went to the cashier, inserted your card, took your card out, and walked out with your items. You kept the card and the new items. The trade of items for money happened only as numbers on a computer screen. You didn't give up anything! You kept your card, and you received new materials. Your card did not reduce in size and your wallet did not get thinner like it does when you pay in cash. It's like the cow farmer telling the chicken farmer that his banker will come by later and make the payment. You're removed from half of the trade because the "value" of the trade is done through another way with no involvement from the purchaser. Removing yourself from a physical trade of goods for goods (milk for eggs or money for items) is dangerous because you don't feel the loss of the trade. The danger increases as the ease and speed of purchases increases with new items like the apple pay or "purchase now" buttons on Amazon.

After attending a family wedding in Los Angeles, California, I was speaking to my 8 yr. old nephew about his upcoming birthday. My nephew began telling me about a new racecar he wanted. These cars are amazing if you're 8. The child sits inside a miniature plastic car that can move when pressing the pedal and drives around slowly for 10 minutes before the battery dies. This racecar was more expensive than the typical birthday gift. Teasingly, I told him cars are expensive and his response made me, and his parents laugh. He said, "it's ok because his parents have a plastic card".

Another story of my own son is when he wanted pizza to be ordered while his mother was cooking dinner. He said, "you can give me your credit card, I'll order what I want, and the rest of the family can eat your dinner".

Both stories demonstrate the disconnect kids have between paying with a credit card and paying for those items later when the bill comes. They see the use of the credit card and believe upon receipt of the item the item has been paid for and they can use it. They don't see the credit card bill arriving the following month. It's all fun and games until the bill arrives. They see the trade as someone gives the store the credit card for a few seconds, they get a pizza, and then someone gives the card back. They miss the real trade because it was done electronically out of their view. Out of everyone's view.

I expect most children go through this phase, especially in today's world where cash is not as common as it once was, but as we grow, the understanding needs to grow as well. Though we do not physically have cash in hand, we are spending our cash value. Without a spending purpose, it's much easier to overspend and lose connection with our value. Financial abstraction describes a theory of purchasing behavior and how it changes because we no longer exchange value by seeing cash leave our accounts. When we paid for everything in cash, we saw the cash leave our wallet and at the end of the day, we could notice when we were running low. Today, spending on a credit card looks no different after full day of shopping. The card might be a bit more worn, our feet are tired, and the car is full of shopping bags, but we have no direct link to the funds we have spent like we did with cash. Credit card companies don't want you to know or feel that connection to the spent value. Credit card companies continually innovate new ways to make it faster and easier to spend money. Innovations such as no longer needing to slide your card but using tap-and-pay. Using Apple Pay or PayPal also are creative ways to make spending less challenging. They like when you become so detached you overspend the limits placed on the card and charge an overage fee.

Why do we have financial abstraction? Today, we jostle between two worlds: the physical world, and the digital world. Both are extremely important, and both have different financial requirements. Many companies have tried to tie the two worlds together, however it's not easy to make life both convenient, user friendly, and safe. In a video game you look at the top of the screen and see a list of all your inventory and cash to spend. Financial abstraction doesn't exist because you instantly see the game value change when a trade is made. In real life we log into an account and determine how much money we have in our account. It can be fast with improved smart phones and apps, but we are still disconnected from our bank account shopping. This disconnects, or lack of ease, opens the door for use to spend without looking at the value we have in our account.

We make purchases in the physical world, but our finances live in the digital world. Credit or debit cards are the link allowing us to move between the two seamlessly, however the cards do not have the ability currently to provide an instant window to the digital world. The blind faith we use when making purchases leads to a false sense of security to buy now and pay for it later. Cards are used because they provide an ease of use. Through a card, you have access to thousands of dollars even if we don't have the ability to pay the bill. We no longer need to carry bundles or cash when staying at a hotel or when purchasing a new car. Now we pay large bills using a single card, instead of counting dollar bills and pennies and paying through the mail. It can be much safer as well. Cards can be shut off if lost or stolen. When cash is stolen, it is gone for good. We don't have a way to turn off cash yet.

Lessons Learned in Financial Abstraction

- Financial Abstraction is when you are removed from the purchaser side of the trade because the trade is completed in a digital world.
- If you don't feel the loss when making a trade, you are more likely to overspend.
- Cash and Cards spend the same value.
- Card companies continually innovate easier ways to spend.
- We spend in the physical world, but our finances live in the digital world.
- A disconnect between the two worlds creates opportunity for us to overspend and lose financial control.

Notes

CHAPTER 6

THE POWER OF MONEY

"Investing isn't about beating others at their game. It's about controlling yourself at your own game."
~ Benjamin Graham – Father of value investing

Money provides an avenue to accomplish great things. Consider your goals for the week, month, or year and there is a very good chance it will take some level of funding to accomplish them. Food, shelter, clothes, cars, vacations, and any other thing you have took money to obtain and whether we like it or not, we don't have an option to walk off into the sunset and live off the land like our ancestors did many years ago. Even those extreme society members who build a life in the wilderness still use money and bartering to obtain the needed living essentials. Society progressed and the common trading item is money as we discussed earlier. Money has an amazing power to create more money if used properly. A common phrase is "it takes money to make money." Obviously, if you let money sit on your table, you cannot expect to come back a day later and have more money sitting on the table, but for now, it is enough to say saving money and not being in debt creates additional ability or power to do great things. Planning and saving small amounts of money each day can create an energy in your life which nothing else can duplicate. You will have money to achieve your dreams. Controlling how you spend your money is powerful and can lead to controlling other aspects of your life, including relationships, advancement opportunities, and peace of mind. If financial freedom is the goal, the proper use of money is the fuel to achieve the goal.

We go to work each day and bring home a paycheck every few weeks. We exchange our time and attention on a specific thing for cash, whether that thing be selling clothes at the mall, fixing luxury cars, or writing code for a tech company. Some of us don't work for other companies but work for ourselves and the same principle exists because our ability to become wealthy doesn't stand on the amount of money we earn or where we earn it. Our ability to become wealthy is determined by our spending habits.

Societies around the world work on the simple exchange principle. We earn money and buy things with money. Just as a dollar is worth what you can buy with that dollar, we often view ourselves as worth the amount of money we can bring home from work. The amount of money we bring in depends on the job we have. Anyone can expect to make about the same wages for mowing grass in one city as the next. I would agree some cities pay higher wages, but those cities are also, most likely, more expensive to live. All things being equal, a person mowing one yard in Denver, Colorado creates the same amount of value as a person mowing a yard in Albany, New York. If I want to make more money, I must change what I can offer. Maybe by adding hedge trimming or edging the yard could increase my worth or value.

While working in the Tech industry, I was based in Salt Lake City, Utah but travelled often to San Jose, California to work on projects. When our team would hire new members, the discussion would ultimately land on where we wanted the position to sit. In Utah or California were often the two options. Those who wanted to stay in the Bay area would often say they would receive a larger salary if they stayed in the Bay area and the Utah residents would say the small salary would go further if they stayed in Utah. Both are right and ultimately get paid the same when we consider the cost of living.

Our society has done a decent job at determining the set price for certain jobs or careers. We can look up the average salary for a medical doctor, a high school teacher, or a night shift security guard. We balance many decisions when we decide the career we want to pursue. Should I go to school for 10 years past high school to become a doctor or should I start my own business instead of going to college. Each decision sets us down a path determining our future. It is our decisions which determine our value we provide to the community. Not only do we make decisions which impact how much money earn, but we also make decisions on how we spend our money. The decisions we make every day determine our value and our future.

The good news is the power of money works the

same for each person, whether you have a lot of money or a limited amount. Money, as a thing, treats all of us equally. We decide how and when to spend it. We decide to either work for our money or make our money work for us. This might sound very strange at first. Making money work for us sounds very complicated and our minds can instantly get overwhelmed with the financial markets and investment trading. I promise, making your money work for you is easier… much easier than those thoughts of investment portfolios and venture funding. You don't need a million dollars in the bank and can even begin when you have more loans than savings. The largest difference between the 1% of the population with the highest income level and much of the remaining population, is the top 1% make their money work for them. Let's look at an example.

When you go to a bank and open a free checking account, have you ever asked yourself why they would do anything for free? They are running a business and doing anything for free doesn't make sense right? What about me is so special, a company would give away one of their main services for FREE? We are special, but not because the bank says so. What they don't tell you is although your account says you have $100 sitting there, that $100 is not actually there. They have taken that money and given it to someone else in a bank loan. But this other person will pay the bank $110 over the next year. You get a free bank account to keep record of your money. The bank gets $100 from you to loan out to other customers. The other customer gets $100 to pay for a house, and then the bank gets the interest on the loan back after a predetermined date. The bank does all this trading to make $10 in the end. Of course, they do this with much larger sums of money with many people and earn great sums of money to grow the business. This is a simple example of the bank making money work for them by gaining interest from your money. So how does an example of a bank making their money work for them relate to us? We are not loaning out money to friends and even if we are, can we ever expect to see that money again? …

Probably not.

When we consider the average household in America has tens of thousands in debt, we can easily see these families spending much of their income to pay only the interest. Paying interest does nothing to reduce the loans or diminish the debt. It is simply the payment made to the debt collector to have the loan. It is a fee saying, I pay you "x interest" amount of dollars just to have the debt. If I pay anything additional after interest, then my principal (loan amount) will go down and my loans will decrease. Over time, these interest payments make up a large portion of the money we make. A great example of this is a 30-year home mortgage. You are extremely excited! You just bought your first home and got a killer rate! 3% fixed rate and you borrowed $200,000. You bought a great home for your small family and can't wait to paint walls and move in your furniture. One afternoon you get a piece of mail from the mortgage company showing your full breakdown of all the payments, interest, and principal, you will make over the next 30 years. It's a lot to take in and then you see the bottom line. The principal amount you will pay off after 30 years is as expected $200,000, but the amount of interest you will pay to the mortgage company is $103,554.90. You quickly add the two and realize you are paying an additional $100K just to have the loan for 30 years. "CROOKS!!" You yell! This must be a mistake. How can so much money be paid when you got such a low interest rate? In fact, this is reality. Even with a low interest rate, over time, we can end up paying so much money just for the privilege of using someone else's money. When you consider other types of loans which hold much higher interest rates, such as credit cards with 25%+ interest rates, we quickly see how we can be spending most of our earned paycheck just for the privilege of using someone's else's money and then still must pay back the principal loan amount. We make our money work for us when we stop paying interest and use the would-be interest money for other things.

Becoming and continuing to remain debt free is the first and easiest way to make out money work for us.

Forget about investing in the foreign trade commissions or balancing a stock portfolio. The easiest way to make our money work for us is to become debt free.

Companies are good at this. They take the money they earn and invest it into other activities that will bring in even more money. As mentioned previously, a bank makes $100 and turns it into $110. Individuals are not so good at this. A common phrase is "I've got money to burn". Life is expensive and we are very good at spending every dime and then some to obtain more and more. We don't allow our earnings to work for us. Instead, we spend everything we've earned leaving nothing behind to work. Often overspending, forcing us to borrow to obtain the additional things we want in life.

I said earlier that money treats us all equally. Just as the bank earned $10 after loaning out $100 to a customer, that customer lost $10 by taking out the loan. This is fair and equal. I also mentioned earlier, leaving money on the table overnight will not produce additional money. Value can only be created through an activity. Not by sitting idle. A bank creates value through finding a person willing to pay $110 back to the bank in one year in exchange for $100 now to use as needed. So how can we make our money work for us like the banks do or the credit card companies? The answer is simple. Avoid unnecessary debt.

When you take out a loan, you are agreeing to payback more than you borrowed. Avoiding debt, such as credit card payments which require a huge interest payment, allows more money to remain in your pocket and can then be used to avoid additional debt later. We can think of this as paying yourself the would-be interest payment. It stays with you to cover future expenses instead of going to the credit card company. Over time, avoiding debt and keeping the would-be interest payments in your account, provides additional wealth which can be used or invested in other activities to increase your value.

The power of money is real. Money is needed to live, but if managed well, your value will increase, and you can begin to accumulate wealth. Just as a train might move slow at first, but after some time and much effort, a train in motion carries great power, almost unstoppable power. Money exists in a similar fashion. Creating wealth starts slowly at first. Saving small amounts is slow progress, however as time passes, avoiding unnecessary purchases, purchasing with purpose, and keeping money in your account and away from interest payments, will cause your value to grow faster and faster. As Wealth accumulates you begin to find investment opportunities to make the power of money work for you instead of against you. As you gain wealth, you find the financial freedom you've dreamed of and an ability to accomplish goals. Just as the train, as time passes and with a bit of effort, you can become unstoppable in financial success with any income.

Lessons Learned in the Power of Money

- Reduce interest payments keeps money in your pocket.
- Small savings now become large savings later.
- Make money work for you instead of working for money.

Notes

CHAPTER 7

MAINTAINING CASHFLOW

"Never take your eyes off the cash flow because it's the
life blood of business."
~ Richard Branson

Cash is king. Whether digital currency or physical, having
funds immediately available provides an advantage when
payment is needed immediately. Not everything can or
should be put on a credit card, and we cannot go to the
bank for a loan for every trip to the grocery store. We
need a certain amount of cash available for everyday
expenses. Even when negotiating for a purchase with a
much higher price tag like a home or a car, having cash
(either digital or physical) provides advantages that can be
used to lower the price. We use cash to make payments
every day. We pay for food, utilities bills, car loan
payments, rent, gas, and entertainment using cash or cash
equivalent like a credit card. We've also talked about the
power that money can bring into your life as it builds
momentum into other investment opportunities. The
power building feature of money is your ability to
managing cashflow.

Why do we call it "cashflow"? There is a motion

relationship between money coming in (income) and money leaving (expenses). Similar to many things in our life, birth and death, rainfall and evaporation, or the flow of a river as water enters and then exits points of the stream. Let's stick to this symbolism of a flowing river to demonstrate what it means to manage your cash flow.

If we look at the Colorado River bordering Nevada and Arizona, USA, along its path is a massive structure called the Hoover Dam. This dam is massive and took five years to complete. It stands taller than the Washington Monument in Washington, D.C at 726 feet holding back enormous amounts of water behind thick walls. Dams are fascinating… Once the infrastructure is complete, there are many benefits to their placement. Hydroelectric power is made when water pass through turbines within the dam structure. The dam stores water for downstream farming irrigation and growing crops. Dams help with flood prevention during periods of heavy rain and with water management during times of drought. Like a dam with water, you and your money can see extreme benefits for the short term and long term if controlled correctly.

I call this "The Dam Model."

First consider 2 key principals to this model

1. Water represents your money and the journey your money takes before you touch it, while you hold it, and after you spend it.
2. The dam and the management of the dam represents the actions you take to manage your cashflow.

Dams are placed along a running river where water is already passing. When the dam is in place, the water gathers into a large body of water usually forming a lake. After spending time collecting in the lake, the water eventually makes it way towards the dam structure. As water enters the dam, it passes through a turbine generating energy and sent out of the dam through port holes. Here, the water continues to flow down the riverbed.

We can think of our money symbolically as the water in "The Dam Model". The dam structure represents the spending habits and the rules we have in place around our spending habits. When water leaves the dam, it is like when we spend money. The water leaves the dam and continues downstream. When we spend money, that money continues down a path from our bank to pay our bills or purchase goods. Our personal financial spending habits or our managing of our money (the dam) regulate the amount of our personal money (water) we spend (leaves the dam) on everything from bills, rent, or dinner out with friends.

Energy turbines are the interesting thing about dams. Dams with no turbines can still be beneficial because they help flood prevention (overspending), but when a dam has turbines, additional long-term benefit is seen. Turbines are used to generate energy which is sold to nearby cities for revenue. For the turbines to spin and create energy, there needs to be sufficient water in reserve held in the lake behind the dam. The turbines will not turn and create electricity with limited water in reserve. Turbines represent activities or investments we do financially with our cash (water) we have in reserve. Relating to our finances, when our money savings are built up, we can then place money into smart investments generating financial 'energy'. We read in almost every financial book out there that the only way to become wealthy or leave a 9-5 job is to stop working FOR MONEY and make your money work FOR YOU. Investments are the way to do that. Whether you invest in stocks, bonds, start a company, or purchase an online business, investments are the only way you go from making money in a job to making money work for you. We can only begin to build wealth and financial freedom when we build up our financial reserve generating energy for additional gain.

This is not a "how to invest" book, but I like to bring up how the financial reserve leads to investments because many who wish to become wealthy want to immediately start a company or jump into the stock market. They want a quick transition to the good life. The life they see every night as they scroll through social media. A quick fix. Bookshelves are full of rags to riches, get-rich-quick ideas, but they are often too good to be true. Any multimillionaire will tell you; consistency is more important to wealth creation than anything else. Consistent and focused effort. Consistent savings. Consistent investments. The consistency of managing our financial dam; knowing the money coming in and money going out provides you confidence and flexibility to make good financial investments. The first step to get to that place is building your financial reserve.

Throughout this book, we talk about savings and strategize on ways to increase your wealth through purposeful spending and increasing savings. Investments are the forward-looking benefit. Once you stop needless spending, avoid financial "death by $20", and live beneath your means, the savings can then be spent on revenue generating assets instead of expenses. We don't dive into the various types of investments in this book because there are thousands of resources out there and it's highly based on your level of risk acceptance, stage of life, and so much more. Here's the secret sauce of investing at any stage of life….

You **cannot** invest in anything if you have no resources to invest.

Only after you control your spending will you then have literally thousands of options available to you.

When the turbines generate power in dam, energy is sold to local communities. When we actively manage our cashflow, we also create enough cash reserve, and our cash turbines turn on creating additional opportunities. They create financial energy and joy but only if we have managed the water correctly and have enough flow to make them function properly. Like a dam manager, you are the manager of your finances. You manage the flow of money coming in, how long it stays with you, and then how it's spent for your benefit. Managing the dam is a full-time job and so is managing your money.

A dam provides benefits upstream and downstream, but the manager must know the quantity of water coming in and the quantity of water leaving for the best overall benefit of the entire river ecosystem. Too little water flow coming in and the turbines don't turn. Too much flow going out and you may run out of water leaving no options for the future with everything downstream drying out. It's a balancing act.

Upstream

The water flowing toward the dam is your income. It's how you bring in finances. A salary or job. More money is represented by a larger river. Your job brings the money where it is collected and could gather if not spent. The lake which usually forms on the back side a dam is resembled as your bank account. Hopefully you can keep money in your account and build more than a puddle before the money goes out the other side.

Great things happen with a good upstream management program. For the dam, the collected water can be used for drinking water in nearby towns and for a recreation spot for many in the area. When you have a lake of cash sitting in a bank account, you reduce the stresses of tomorrow if an unexpected expense comes your direction because you now have a reserve.

The Dam

The dam represents your cashflow management and your spending habits. The dam holds back the water allowing it to collect into the lake. Your spending habits monitor how much money leaves or stays. Reducing spending holds back the money allowing it to collect into a larger pool of savings. Life is expensive and requires payment of bills. A dam must always release enough water to maintain the life downstream. Similarly, bills need to be paid to keep the lights on and food needs to be purchased to sustain life. A dam with good rules helps to build up the savings lake as well as better manage activities and expenses downstream.

The Energy Turbines

The energy turbines are within the walls of the dam. They need the force of a large amount of water rushing through to create enough power. When the amount of water behind the dam is large enough, you can control the correct amount of water that goes through the turbines before exiting downstream. The turbines represent investments you can make because you've built up the savings by reducing your spending habits. Investing creates additional opportunities for growth and revenue just as a dam sells the energy it creates and creates additional cash flow.

Downstream

The water moving downstream represents the money spent to sustain your life. The needs and the wants. For the dam, the water has been released and sent downstream to continue providing for wildlife or other ecological systems just as any other river does. Financially, the money released from the bank account is sent "downstream" to pay bills like rent, gas, food, or a movie night with friends.

Until we die, and maybe a short time after we die, there are bills to pay. This is why I like the image of a dam so well. A dam controls the amount of water released but it doesn't stop it. As in life, we need to control our money leaving our account. Notice I did not say to stop it completely. Life takes money and we need to spend it to live. The quantity of money leaving is controllable though.

Managing the Dam

We are the managers of our financial dam. We know the amount of water coming from upstream and we need more coming in than leaving to build up the lake behind our dam. I'm sure the Hoover Dam runs on a set of rules or guidelines to ensure the dam is properly maintained and appropriately controls the water upstream and downstream for maximum benefit. When considering the rules of our financial dam, below are a few I recommend...

Rule #1 – Running a dam properly takes a team.

The financial impact of controlling the money flow is a coordination of everyone on the dam team. You cannot manage the dam alone, especially when the flow of money is done by multiple people. A consistent reason for stress in any relationship can be financial. Talk about the plan and determine together how to best manage both the upstream financial income as well as the downstream financial expenses. There may be many managers running the dam and all perspectives are important.

Rule #2 – You cannot just turn the dam off

You cannot turn off the dam without serious consequences like flooding and serious damage to equipment. The same goes in a financial dam. Trying to just turn off the dam will lead to missed payments and serious financial problems. Living a life requires expenses. There are however levers and buttons to press in a planned sequence allowing you to slow the flow of money leaving the dam. Reducing expenses, stopping subscriptions, or paying off loans will allow you to slow the flow of water leaving your dam and grow the financial lake behind the dam. Just remember, shutting off one port hole and opening another does not build savings.

Rule #3 – The right balance between upstream flow and downstream flow is challenging.

Seasons alter the quantity of water coming into the lake behind the dam. Seasons of life also change the quantity of money coming into our life. Changing jobs, obtaining pay increases, family emergencies, and others change our financial river flow. You, as the dam manager need to adjust the outflow of water consistent with the inflow of water. You maintain the balance. You need to adjust your expenses as your income may change. As we discussed, the world is doing everything possible to separate you from your money. They want more water for themselves and do not care about the dam. energy for turbines, or anyone else. They only want more water. You need to balance the money coming in with the water leaving. Maintaining the balance takes effort.

Using a budget or finance professional can help predict the flow of money and help predict periods of financial drought or when financial rainfall will come.

Rule #4 – There is always the want for more water downstream.

Entities downstream always scream for more water. Farmers want more water for their crops or ecosystems would be beautifully green with additional water. As in finance, there are always more projects or more fun items we can spend our money on. I cannot go to any business without being asked to donate to a great cause. I want to support them all but supporting them all would have a horrible effect on my savings. The extra fun or additional support is powered only when you have enough of a reserve to power your financial turbines. If you allow too much water to go to expenses downstream, you will not have enough water in reserve powering turbines.

Rule #5 – Dams take time to build and time for water to fill the reserve.

Anything worthwhile takes time to build correctly. Dams can take years or decades of planning and building before the benefits are seen. Just because you are not managing a fully developed dam today doesn't mean you cannot begin making moves today to put yourself in a better position in the future. It takes time, but the result is financial freedom. Even if your river is small and only a trickle at this point, you will see the benefit of building a dam now as your river grows into a great lake and downstream ecosystem. The full development of upstream activities, energy creation through turbines, and downstream activities take time. The great news is you are not building from scratch. You can use examples of others to help establish your rules for success.

Lessons Learned in the Dam Model

- Managing money means thinking about money coming in and going out
- You cannot invest in anything if you have no resources to invest.
- There is always a demand for more water downstream.
- You are the manager of the entire operation.
- It takes a team to manage the dam properly.

Notes

CHAPTER 8

SHOPPER'S DILEMMA

"Our jobs as marketers are to understand how the
customer wants to buy and help them do so."
~ Bryan Eisenberg

As I was in the grocery store a little while ago, I saw a
negotiation between a child and a mother that I am
positive everyone can relate to as either being the child,
the parent, or just an observer in a store. The child and
mother were in the cereal aisle. As they entered the aisle I
noticed the boy trying to jump out of the shopping cart.
The mother reluctantly let him down and he rushed over
to the most colorful box of cereal. Grabbing the box and
rushing over to his mother asking if they could buy it. She
grabs it and places it in the cart. The young boy screams
with delight right before his eyes land on the next large
colorful box of sugary cereal with some well-known
cartoon character and rainbows jumping across the cover.
I also laugh as I see mothers replacing the colorful boxes
when the child turns their back. A parent must do what a
parent must do, right?

As a child, I remember placing a few treats in the
cart when my mother was not looking hoping she would

just buy it when we got to checkout. Now as an adult I find my own children doing the same thing. The sneaky shelf grabs can be frustrating but understanding why this happens is even more frustrating because all these actions by children are planned by marketers. These companies know those items which attract children to products and make sure they are within eyeline of the kids.

Companies who sell products conduct mountains of research to target different types of buyers. Buyers including babies, infants, teenagers, young adults, middle age, and seniors. They target the various races, genders, income levels, political preferences, and any other way to dissect a population. Product sales are highly determined by data. Even distribution of products to various areas of the U.S. are determined by marketing data. This is why you can only find certain brands in specific regions.

In most grocery stores, the sugary junk cereal is placed within eye level of a small child and healthy cereal is placed within eye level of adults. This is because the cereal company is planning on the 8-year-old kid walking down the aisle looking for their favorite box and eye level is easier to see than the top shelf. The same is true for adults. If you were to go through every aisle, this same principle applies. Every single item in the store is specifically placed to sell it the most effectively way.

You, as the customer need to be aware of the professional marketer's game. They are trying to separate you from your money. They are good at making products easy to find and easy to buy. They are also good at your path in the store to walk past the candy aisle if the only thing you want is milk. Have you noticed every time you need milk, you walk to the very back side of the store and pass almost everything else offered in the store? Have you also noticed, an item with a bright yellow or red "sale" sticker on it? Why is it bright red or yellow? It makes it stand out and catches your eye. If the sale sticker is dark blue, you would not be able to see it from across the store!

Historically, research into the types of people who buy certain products has been done through focus groups. A company wants to see who buys product "x" and they test different types of buyers to see which buyer type would be most successful to focus on. Today, more and more of this research is being done through online sales or promotional programs. If you have ever been asked at the checkout counter if you would like to sign up for a store card, the company will provide you a possible deal for signing up, but they receive your information on all your purchases. Companies are getting so good at knowing your buying habits and predicting the products you need even before you realize it.

There is one story marketing story told in every marketing class across the globe to prove this point and to add some humor showing how these companies use this data to drive future sales. The truth of the story is unknown, though I'm sure it could be possible. It goes like this…

One day, a dad came home from work and checked the mailbox. He found the traditional bills, but he found something new and very interesting. Inside his mail he found a promotional pamphlet in his teenage daughter's name. He had seen these pamphlets in her name before, but they usually were for summer clothes or new tech devices. This pamphlet was different. It was for baby clothes and diapers. The father was very upset and thought this must be a mistake! She is just a teenager and should not be sent advertisements for baby clothes and diapers. Maybe this was for his wife, and they were pregnant again, but he had not known. Upset the pamphlet was sent to his house in his daughter's name, the father called the store and demanded an apology. Customer service agents apologized for the mail sent in his daughter's name and was told it must have been a mistake. He was told the pamphlets are computer generated from algorithms and are based on historic purchases and purchases made by others who have looked at or purchased similar items on their website and other data points. He was told the pamphlets can be wrong and there would be nothing to worry about and the store promptly removed the daughters name from their mailing list. Satisfied, the father threw away the diaper pamphlet and went about his day. A few days later, he was approached by his wife and daughter and told his daughter is expecting a child and they would need to start shopping for baby stuff. The computers where accurate in predicting the needs of their customers.

Be aware of intentions to entice additional purchases. Just being aware can stop a few purchases each day saving hundreds of dollars each week. Companies do not want you to save money, as this means you are not spending money in their stores.

Here in, rests the "Shopper's Dilemma". You must go shopping for clothes, food, entertainment, and everything else you use in your daily life. Shopping is easy and you have many choices whether that be the mall or your favorite store or the local supermarket, or online. The online ads make these same problems for shoppers. The dilemma is how do you save money if everything in this world is targeted toward separating you from your money. How can we go against such a grand effort by professionals working long days in the office, in fact, teams of people focusing on how to entice you to buy their product? You can avoid many regrettable purchases if you just acknowledge the game marketers are playing. Knowing how marketers are targeting you and recognizing the marketer's manipulation in stores or online can be tricky at first, but over time, it becomes very easy to detect.

My wife and I now laugh at some of the ways we are targeted. One day we were walking around a local supermarket where we spotted a $5 bin of movies where the advertisement said every movie in the bin was $5. We both grew up spending many nights watching movies with our families and have fond memories of those evenings. Most of the movies were classic movies from our childhood. We quickly began looking through the bin and uncovered many movies we would like to own and enjoy watching. After a few minutes we both had a handful of movies. All in about $50 worth of movies that we wanted to watch. We looked at each other and just started laughing. $5 each adds up very quickly when you view the movies as classics and believe you must have them. When we walked into the store, we had no intention of buying movies and only considered it once we saw the bin. They were such a great deal we felt the need to check it out. Had we discussed earlier that morning we would be spending $50 on movies that day, we would have scoffed and said we don't need more movies and we don't have the money to buy $50 in movies. However, once we entered the store, we suddenly felt the need to pick them up and spend the money. Why the change? Did we not know our own needs or was it the store's marketing efforts trying to convenience us of our needs? That night, the store did a great job through marketing efforts to play to our emotions. Even though we didn't plan on buying movies that night, as soon as we saw them, we felt we had to have them.

The bins were placed in the middle of the aisle. From a functional standpoint, it makes no sense to place a bin directly in the middle of the supermarket walkway. For marketers, this is the perfect place for high profit, emotional purchases. Love at first sight can be great and long lasting, but purchase at first sight can be expensive and full of regrets! There was no prior thought to the purchase. My wife and I fell hard for the purchase at first thought while looking at the $5 movie bin. After a few minutes of digging, we both looked up at the same time and said, "Death by $20". We got marketed but were lucky enough avoid purchasing the movies we did not need and did not plan on buying. Don't get me wrong, I have purchased movies and we still enjoy a good movie with the family. Making sure we go into the store with the intention on buying a movie is key to maintaining control of our finances and not buying on impulse. By doing so we maintain control during the Shopper's Dilemma.

<u>Lessons Learned in the Shopper's Dilemma</u>

- Marketers place items in a store for the best chance of a sale. They know your shopping habits and plan accordingly.
- Knowing the marketing game makes you aware of how to avoid unnecessary purchases.

<u>Notes</u>

CHAPTER 9

REPEAT SHOPPING

"Repetition of the same thought or physical action
develops into a habit which, repeated frequently
enough, becomes an automatic reflex."
~Normal Vincent Peale

We have all done it. We plan and journey to a store for
something specific. We're not drifting between aisles, and
we may even have a list! We hit each section of the store
like a ninja, and we glide in and out quickly. We are
excited because so much time was saved and now, we
have the entire day to ourselves... That is until we realize
we forgot three items on our list. We rush home with the
items and as we walk into our home, someone go "hey
did you remember...?" WE FORGOT SOMETHING!!!
Our plans are ruined! We don't know how it happened,
but it did and now we have to load the car back up and
head back to the store.

We're not happy being back at the store and now
start to lose the composure and determination to stick to
our original list we had during the first trip and begin to
deviate from the list. Things are heading south quickly!
We make the return trip and start thinking about making

this second trip "worth all the effort". Adding things to the shopping cart which were off the original list quickly adds up and where we once were doing great not adding unnecessary items, we now have a cart of things never intended to be on the list. Ten dollars here, and fifteen dollars there makes one small mistake into a much larger one. We find humor and chuckle at this story because we've all done this and it will probably happen more than enough times in the future as well, but we don't need to blow our budget when this happens.

I've seen men have this happen to them over and over. Men are known for repeat shopping when they go to a home improvement store. A few months ago, I fell into the same situation while doing a simple home improvement project. The initial goal was to get some silicone spray to stop my garage door from make that horrible squeaking noise when opening and closing. I was worried my neighbor would begin to think I held a tortured animal in my garage because the sound the door would make during each opening. To stop the noise, I needed to spray the hinges with this silicone spray. A simple and inexpensive fix, right?

I went to the store, got the spray and while completing the project, I realized I needed a replacement wheel for the garage door. I didn't know I needed this part until I got into the project, but regardless, I was heading back to the store for a second time. I was frustrated and ready to be done with this simple project and having to go to the store for the second time was annoying. The project was supposed to be very simple and take, at most 10 minutes. Now, I was spending an entire afternoon fixing this problem. As I enter the store, I'm frustrated and a bit embarrassed hoping nobody working at the store recognizes that I was just there. I know, I know, it's dumb to think that but I do. I felt I needed to make the most out of this second trip. I kept thinking about all the other small projects needed to be completed and did not want to come back to the store AGAIN to get more stuff. This time I made sure I gathered enough items to complete not only the first garage door project but multiple projects. I left with a bag full of items, including, the replacement wheel for the garage, a large wrench, duct tape, an oil pan, and a few other tools. I left spending $80. This second trip made a simple 10-minute project with a budget of $10 dollars turned into a 3-hour project with a final cost of $90 dollars because I spent money on parts not originally in my plan.

We go to the store almost every day, yet it is not an easy venture. This is especially true if you have a mini-van full of children or a long day ahead. Going to the store can become such a chore at times. By the time we walk through the front doors, we are lucky to remember half of the items we originally needed. This is why many families meander through each aisle hoping to remember what they need when they see it. The meander method works a little too well, so we rely on this method because it becomes easier to meander than to plan and prepare. We grab more than originally planned and end up with a larger bill at checkout.

One Saturday morning in late 2016, my wife and I decided we would go to the grocery store together. At the time, we had a one-year-old son and anyone with small children knows the difficulty shopping with them it's an entirely new challenge and could be its own "how-to" book. We made it to the store and did not have a plan. As we normally did at the time, we started on the right side of the store, with all the breads and picked up items as we remembered them. We went down almost every aisle remembering things as we saw them. And then it happened! The kid started to lose his mind! Crying, and reaching for shelved items and no matter what we gave him, he wanted more. Even with a second pair of hands, all three of us started to become frustrated and we started to quickly go down the aisles picking up even more items not on the list. The situation became so crazy we decided to cut the visit short and purchase the items in our basket and my wife would come back later while I stayed home watching our son. When she went back to the store later, as anyone would do, she started over back at the bread section. She didn't repurchase everything, but even more items were purchased because she had to go back to the store a second time.

This story is funny to look back on. It illustrates a few mistakes of managing expenses. We went into the store without a plan. That was the first mistake. Not having a plan caused the second mistake by wondering down the aisles trying to remember if we "had tuna at home or should we get some while we are here". There's no way to remember everything you have in the pantry, so it's no wonder how more items are picked up than needed. I would imagine all of us have had the experience of buying something we thought we needed only to arrive home and see a brand-new box we forgot about sitting in our pantry. We put them together and just move on. The third and final mistake was heading back to the store to complete the shopping. The frustration is still present during the second trip and will again lead to unnecessary purchases and additional unplanned costs.

The habit of picking more things up when we repeat shop can be beat, but it takes practice and dedication to the budget. During a stint between jobs, I worked for a property manager doing odd jobs around the complex. The property manager would stop by a home improvement store every day (sometimes multiple times each day) to pick up only the parts he needed for the repairs for that day. He was a perfect example of a repeat shopper. The big difference was we always went with a plan knowing exactly what he needed. Each time I went with him to help lift drywall or pick up wood boards he never meandered and only picked up specific items he needed. He never deviated from his list even if his list was only in his head. It was incredible!

The repeat shopping principle is easy…

- Step 1: Make a plan before shopping.
- Step 2: Avoid returning to the store if possible.
- Step 3: If returning to the store, remain calm and stick to the original plan.

Avoid going to the store multiple times and you will avoid unnecessary spending. Inevitably, we will return to the store because we forgot something, or a part was needed we didn't know about until well into the project. The key is to know this will happen, not become frustrated, and stick to the original plan. Grabbing items to make the most of our time leads to "Death by $20" purchases and leads to overspending. Marketers are great at product placement. They know our spending habits because of data analysis, but we also know our spending habits and can fight back. Don't fall in love with products at first sight and make an emotional purchase. Don't do it! You went to the store the first time with a plan. When you repeat shop, do just that… repeat the plan and don't deviate from it.

Lessons Learned in the Repeat Shopping

- Go to the store with a plan to avoid unnecessary purchases.
- If you need to return for another item, go back with another plan.
- Aisle meandering is not a plan and leads to unnecessary purchases.

Notes

CHAPTER 10

EVERYTHING'S ON SALE

"We better get it now on sale! It might be gone
tomorrow" …
~Everyone at some point in our life

We've all said these words to convince ourselves to buy something now instead of waiting to buy it later. We see sales in stores every day. 5% off, 10% off, Buy One Free – Get One, Blowout Sales, Going Out of Business, are all lines used to attract customers. Have you ever stopped and asked why they put items on sale? Have you ever wondered why the "Sale" sign in the window has been there for 7 months and in fact has some dust on it from sitting in one place for so long? There are, what I call "real" sales and "fake" sales in stores every day and in every season.

Allow me to demonstrate exactly what I mean when I say "real" or "fake" sales. Luke went to a store one day, of a well-known brand. He was in the area and had time to look around so he went in because the window had a huge "Everything must go" and "Closing soon sale" signs in the window They set the trap and he took the bait. Luke was heading in and started looking through their jacket section. After a few racks he noticed lots of boxes around the store full of new clothes. In fact, the store was a mess and many of the employees were scrambling to unpack and organize the store, but the manager just kept moving more boxes from the back into the front of the store. He became interested and made a comment about a closing store is hard to manage with so many clothes to sell with a limited time to sell them. Luke was referring to the "Closing Soon" sign he read in the front of the window. The manger looked confused for just a second and then said the boxes are not inventory from the back, but a new truck shipment of new product they were putting out on the floor. Being confused because of the sign in the window, Luke asked about why they would purchase more clothes if they were closing soon. The manger then began to explain during a low season, the store entices customers to come in the store using the sign and in fact had no intention to close the store. Being a little annoyed that he'd fallen for the marketing trick to get him into the store, the manager laughed and said, "every store is closing soon in some way or another, especially if no customers come into the store.". Luke thought it was a clever way to market but also a little dishonest. The store had no plans to close, but only to "out discount" other stores and entice additional customers into their store.

This is a "fake" sale.

Fake sales list extreme discounts year-round and you can always ask, "50% from what original price?". More than likely the item was NEVER available or even listed for the original price but immediately placed on sale for only the appearance of a sale. Anyone can say the price of a candy bar is $100.00 originally and then claim a 98% off sale. You are still buying the candy bar for $2. Is it a great deal because you got a 98% discount? NO! The original price was outrageous. You only save money if you would have made the purchase at the original price without a sale. When comparing the two prices you would have made the purchase, only then is the sale saving you money. If you would have only made the purchase as a 'discounted' rate, then you only valued the object at that discounted price and it cost you the price you paid.

This is a challenging topic because everyone loves to save money, but the term "look how much money I saved" touches some deep part of my soul and I cringe every time I hear it. Especially when they are carrying two arms full of items from the store. I even fall into the trap and annoy myself when I say I bought something on sale and 'saved' money. I understand the phrase is used to mean we bought it on a good deal, but you didn't 'save' any money! You purchased something and you actually paid the price you thought was fair and the price the store thought was fair. Remember the Shopper's Dilemma? Marketer's entire job is to dream up new tactics to separate you from your money. Always remember the stores are not putting an item on sale because they are our friends. The store would prefer to sell at a higher price because it would make the store more profitable and probably lead to a high pay raise or bonus. Purchasing the item at a higher price would benefit their financials and make the store better off. The manager would probably be promoted if they sold more items at a higher price, however they understand inventory management is critical and want to move inventory which has been sitting idle and one way to get it sold and moved out is to drop the price and make the value favorable for more people. The store gets the product moved out while still making a small profit, and we get the satisfaction of feeling we got a good deal.

Herein rests my issue with "saving" money when buying something on sale. Rarely, are the items we need to purchase found on sale. Bread, milk, and other staples of life rarely go on sale and if they do, it usually is because of an expiration date soon to lapse, and the discount is minimal. Bottom line… the items we purchase daily don't go on sale because the store manager knows they don't need to put it on sale to make the sale. No matter if it is regular priced or on sale, customers purchase the same amount every week. The sales are predictable. Because of this, they are enticed to keep the price at the original amount and manage inventory based on historic sales data.

The items which we find on sale are the impulse purchases. Sale items are emotional buys. The items customers would normally not consider picking up, but once we see the giant red letters "SALE", it catches our attention and we think, "look at that price, they are practically giving me the item for free". Ask yourself... Would you make this purchase if listed only at the original price tag? If no, then there are no true savings. The alternative to you buying the item on sale was not buying it at all. Instead of spending $0, you've now spent $20. Extra money spent. So, we didn't save money. We spent more money than was planned.

I will concede the point that if (and only if) we are already considering making a purchase at the original price and then find that item on sale, we have saved money. In my experience, this rarely happens. We purchase more items not intended because of a "For Sale" sign than the experience of walking into a store to make a purchase only to find that same item on sale.

Anyway, let's continue to talk about becoming aware of "real" vs. "fake" sales. One of the easiest things to do is keep your eyes open and notice items which seem to constantly have "year-end blowouts" or "now only" or some other ridiculous logo aimed to attract buyers. A perfect example for me has always been car dealerships and mattress store fronts. They ALWAYS have huge flags and signs declaring the largest sales of the year. I mean seriously... every holiday of the year, even the odd ones that nobody celebrates begin with "LARGEST SALE OF THE YEAR!!!"

Fake Sale

During Memorial Day in the US, or any holiday for that matter, TV and radio commercials are full of car adds and they all are the same.

> "Come and see our selection! All these cars NEED to be moved off our lots IMMEDIETLY and we are giving the customer the biggest sale of the CENTURY."

If the sale is the biggest of the century, then next year, the sale should be bigger than the previous year, but it's not. All over the country, stores claim to have the largest sale or the biggest blowout. I even saw an electronics store have a "going out of business" sign on their window for about 2 years until finally they closed their doors. I've seen stores fixing "going out of business" signs permanently in attempts to attract buyers looking for large discounts. It works because everyone wants to get a good price, right?

The marketing game is to do whatever it takes to get you to come into the store and look around. Once you're inside, the chance of a customer conversion is high by purchasing items at first sight. If the signs in the front can make you think there are better deals than a similar store across the street the marketing team has done their job. There are no rules to the signs and what the meaning of the signs must be. The largest sale of the century could be an opinion of the owner. It doesn't have to be the largest sale of the century for the store to rise the giant flag claiming the sale. I'm pretty sure the largest century sale flag is just one of many they keep rolled up in the back-storage room where during a certain week of the year, they go back, get it out, and hoist it up the flagpole.

Candy is another example as the seasons may change, we always see a "buy 2 bags for $7, or 1 bag for $5" signs. The signs are so permanent on the shelf they collect dust. I fall for this trick too often but mostly because I know I will go through 1 bag and wish I had a second bag. The candy may change based on the holiday, but the fake sales stay the same. Speaking of candy… I've heard candy corn is the #1 sold candy for Halloween. Why does this happen? It's gross, chalky, and need to stop. Seriously… stop.

Car dealerships are a funny example of a "fake" sale because no matter the holiday, month, celebration, or other excited weekday you walk into a dealership, there is always an advertised big deal. Between the over-the-top commercials literally yelling "COME ON DOWN" (making me feel like a Price is Right contestant) or the giant colorful squiggly air machine creatures in the parking lot, I just can't take them seriously. The enticements slightly change, but a deal is always available. To be fair, there are "real" deals happening at dealerships all the time, but it is on an individual car or dealership basis. These deals are not on the marketing advertisement level. Certainly not only because it is Labor Day.

Real Sale

Let's reexamine the car dealership. I mentioned dealerships can have real sales, but it exists on an individual level. Many dealerships are more negotiable to drop the price if you look for a car near the end of the month. The dealership management needs to meet monthly sales quotas to remain in business or meeting monthly goals. The real sale happens when the seller (company or dealership) is enticed to give you a discount from the original purchase price and this discount does not happen every day or on a regular basis. At the end of the month, the dealership management needs to meet sales numbers and if the final sales price is something positive, management is enticed to lower the price.

Another example of a real sale is the end of season sales for ski equipment or biking equipment. I lived in the Rocky Mountains for a while and saw this each March for ski equipment and each November for biking equipment. At the end of either season rental shops give steep discounts on the previous seasons' equipment. They know next season customers will want newer equipment and the older equipment will sit, so they get what they can for it now or it will be worth nothing next season. This is a real sale. The company is enticed to sell you equipment at a discount and the sale is not happening year-round or on a regular basis. It only happens once the season has ended, and they have a large quantity of remaining inventory they want to sell quickly.

Buying equipment on sale at the end of the season does not mean you 'saved money' though. You only save money if you would have made the purchase at the original price. The fact you waited to buy end of season goods probably means you were not willing to make the purchase at the original price. Buying equipment at the end of season is a great tactic to use when you want to spend less on great gear only a season old. I love this stuff because it shows you care about your value of money. You see the value of that item as only worth the lesser price tag. In the end though, you still paid an agreed upon price with the seller and it <u>cost</u> you money.

Real and fake sales are enticing but to take advantage and reduce your spending we need to pay attention to the reason behind the sale.

Look at the sale from the marketer point of view.

- Why are they putting the item on sale?
- Was the original price tag a price any reasonable person would pay for this item?

Then we can look at the sale from our (the purchaser point of view).

- Would I make the purchase at the original price?
- Was I already looking to buy this item before it went on sale?

- Do I value this item at the current price regardless of a 'sale'.

We as the purchaser have no advantage making a purchase during a fake sale. The opposite is true when we purchase during a real sale. Real sales provide us an opportunity to make a planned purchase at a much lower price. Thus, truly saving money and reducing our outflow of money.

Lessons Learned in Everything is on Sale

- Beware of fake sales which provide no savings.
- Real sales are available with actual savings but not just because you showed up.
- Real sales exist because of a benefit to the seller. Recognize that benefit and negotiate from that position.
- Saying you bought something and "saved" money are contradictory statements.
- Planning can really help to avoid falling for a fake sale.

Notes

CHAPTER 11

ACTIVELY MANAGING YOUR MONEY

"If you want to see the sunshine, you have to weather the storm."
~ Frank Lane

Every time I go bowling, I stand at the machine entering names and the question always comes up… "Do you want the bumpers up or down?". You've seen it before… the bumpers at a kid's birthday party that prevent a bowling ball from entering the gutter. Instead of entering the gutter, the ball bounces off the bumpers like a pinball down the lane and hits a few pins usually providing a moment of complete joy to a 4-year-old. Without the bumper the party would be a bit of a downer with scores probably not breaking 10. Believing I'm somewhat of a bowling prodigy (obviously forgetting about my last bowling performance) I always scoffingly, I select down. I probably even mumble under my breath "bumpers are for kids".

Selecting a ball from the public rack a few pounds heavier than needed, I start heaving the ball as fast as I can down the lane. For some unknown reason, I believe when the ball hits the pins, the pins will explode, leaving no chance any pins will be left remaining. It's not long before my arm is a bit sore, and I've sent many throws into the gutter and seen too many pins left standing. It's always when I'm mad at myself that I notice two or three lanes at the end of the alley where I see little kids bowling with the bumpers.

Oh! I should have selected the bumpers!

At first the bumpers seem foolish, but now they are genius! Even the youngest child whose bowling ball barely makes it down the lane knocks a few down.

We go through a similar reaction when we talk about budgets. At first, we believe we are fine without it. We don't need it. We are adults and budgets are for kids who sell lemonade at the street corner or only for big corporations who report quarterly financials to shareholders. I know what I can spend, and I don't need help guiding my decisions. Just as my bowling decision to add bumpers came too late to help my bowling score, we also need to make an early decision to create and follow a budget. Waiting too long to implement and follow a budget can really affect our financial score. No matter where you currently are, the sooner you create and follow a budget, the sooner your financials will be better.

Financially, a budget acts as the bumpers to our spending habits. Do we spend like I bowl?; throwing the ball as fast as we can, hoping to crush the pins only to end up in the gutter? Or do we spend as the kids bowl, using the bumpers to guide the ball all the way down the lane smashing into the pins and ultimately leading to a loud high pitch scream of happiness?

If you're like me, I hate the word "Goals" or "Budgets". They sound dull and boring. They also sound like someone is trying to tell me what I should and should not do with the money. Since grade school. Every teacher and mentor asked the unanswerable question "What are your goals?". I never had a good answer. I always thought my goals were to pass the class or just make it through the work week alive.

It was only when I started to ask this question to others who I coached or mentored that I found my own answers and it came from understanding two principles.

1. You need directional heading to start any journey.
2. journey is made up of many tangible actions between here and there.

What those asking the question really want to know is "where do you see yourself heading?" or "where do you want to be in the future?". Once that is established, they should always follow up with a question asking, "what you are doing NOW to eventually get to a desirable future position?". If a high school student wants to become a doctor, a good mentor would tell them to observe or volunteer in hospitals while attending college and obtain a science 4-year degree. Tangible actions along the journey. There is a roadmap to achieve the goal. If a person wants to run a marathon in under 4 hours, they need to ask themselves "what do I need to do now, so come race day, I will achieve my goal?". For many people, everything we do in life requires action now if we want to be in a specific position in the future. Put in the work now, and a reward usually follows.

Finances are no different. If the goal is to have financial freedom, what are you doing <u>NOW</u> to put yourself in that desirable position later? A budget is nothing more than a plan or roadmap to achieve that desirable future state. If done correctly and according to your needs, a well followed budget can get you through tough economic swings, job loss, family adjustments, and provide flexibility during good times. Most importantly for me, a well thought out and thorough budget provides peace of mind. However, the best plan not followed, leads nowhere.

A budget sets limits and protects the value you have created for yourself and your family. Just as the bowling lane example, some spenders (bowlers) need more help than others. Budgets can be as specific or as general as your needs demand and there are no one size fits all budgets. Our lives are different, and thus each of our budgets will be different. I will present three varied types of budgeting I have used at different times in my life and attempt to provide context to why the type of budget was the best option at the time. Adapting the type of budget to your situation will lead to the best outcome. Very simply, the three types of budgets are:

1. Highly Monitored Budget
2. Medium Monitored Budget
3. Low Monitored Budget

Highly Monitored Budget

In 2009, I was about to enter my senior year of college and was very excited, but I was also very apprehensive. Heading into that year, my funds were extremely low. Lower than any previous start to a college year. To graduate on time, the previous summer I had to take a class which cut into my hours at my job. I felt the financial pressure and had a to make some spending adjustments. If I did not set a highly monitored budget, I would be sunk and run out of money. Every dollar was precious, and I needed to make sure every dollar was spent wisely.

I started by separating my expenses into multiple categories. I separated my costs into mandatory expenses I had to pay each month and non-mandatory expenses each month. This showed my needs versus to wants and forced myself to take hard look at my true needs and my wants. My needs included, car (gas & maintenance), food (groceries), cell phone bill, education (tuition, books, job search costs), Living (rent, gas, electrical, water, cleaning), and hygiene (soap, shampoo, razors, shaving cream, etc.). My wants then came next. This included entertainment (movies, outings with friends, etc.), new clothes, dating, food (out to eat), and savings. It looked something like the below excel layout.

Budget Highly Monitored

Income

Starting Money Available	$ 10,000.00	August	September	October	November	December	January	Feburary	March	April	May
Anticipated Income		$200.00	$200.00	$200.00	$200.00	$200.00	$200.00	$200.00	$200.00	$200.00	$200.00
Student Loans		$3,500.00	$0.00	$0.00	$0.00	$0.00	$3,500.00	$0.00	$0.00	$0.00	$0.00
TOTAL		$3,700.00	$200.00	$200.00	$200.00	$200.00	$3,700.00	$200.00	$200.00	$200.00	$200.00

Expenses

Mandatory Cost		August	September	October	November	December	January	Feburary	March	April	May
Car	gas	($80.00)	($80.00)	($80.00)	($80.00)	($80.00)	($80.00)	($80.00)	($80.00)	($80.00)	($80.00)
	maintenance	($25.00)	($25.00)	($25.00)	($25.00)	($25.00)	($25.00)	($25.00)	($25.00)	($25.00)	($25.00)
Food	groceries	($200.00)	($200.00)	($200.00)	($200.00)	($200.00)	($200.00)	($200.00)	($200.00)	($200.00)	($200.00)
Cell Phone	bill	($55.00)	($55.00)	($55.00)	($55.00)	($55.00)	($55.00)	($55.00)	($55.00)	($55.00)	($55.00)
Education	tuition	($3,500.00)	$0.00	$0.00	$0.00	$0.00	($3,500.00)	$0.00	$0.00	$0.00	$0.00
	books	($600.00)	$0.00	$0.00	$0.00	$0.00	($600.00)	$0.00	$0.00	$0.00	$0.00
	job hunting	($25.00)	($25.00)	($25.00)	($25.00)	($25.00)	($25.00)	($25.00)	($25.00)	($25.00)	($25.00)
Living	rent	($400.00)	($400.00)	($400.00)	($400.00)	($400.00)	($400.00)	($400.00)	($400.00)	($400.00)	($400.00)
	gas	($60.00)	($60.00)	($60.00)	($60.00)	($60.00)	($60.00)	($60.00)	($60.00)	($60.00)	($60.00)
	electrical	($50.00)	($50.00)	($50.00)	($50.00)	($50.00)	($50.00)	($50.00)	($50.00)	($50.00)	($50.00)
	water	($25.00)	($25.00)	($25.00)	($25.00)	($25.00)	($25.00)	($25.00)	($25.00)	($25.00)	($25.00)
	cleaning supplies	($15.00)	($15.00)	($15.00)	($15.00)	($15.00)	($15.00)	($15.00)	($15.00)	($15.00)	($15.00)
	Hygiene	($10.00)	($10.00)	($10.00)	($10.00)	($10.00)	($10.00)	($10.00)	($10.00)	($10.00)	($10.00)
TOTAL		($5,045.00)	($945.00)	($945.00)	($945.00)	($945.00)	($5,045.00)	($945.00)	($945.00)	($945.00)	($945.00)

Non Madatory Costs		August	September	October	November	December	January	Feburary	March	April	May
Entertainment	Movies	($10.00)	($10.00)	($10.00)	($10.00)	($10.00)	($10.00)	($10.00)	($10.00)	($10.00)	($10.00)
	Outings with Friends	($25.00)	($25.00)	($25.00)	($25.00)	($25.00)	($25.00)	($25.00)	($25.00)	($25.00)	($25.00)
New Clothes	Clothes	($50.00)	($50.00)	($50.00)	($50.00)	($50.00)	($50.00)	($50.00)	($50.00)	($50.00)	($50.00)
Dating	Dates	($40.00)	($40.00)	($40.00)	($40.00)	($40.00)	($40.00)	($40.00)	($40.00)	($40.00)	($40.00)
Savings	Savings	$0.00	$0.00	$0.00	$0.00	$0.00	$0.00	$0.00	$0.00	$0.00	$0.00
TOTAL		($125.00)	($125.00)	($125.00)	($125.00)	($125.00)	($125.00)	($125.00)	($125.00)	($125.00)	($125.00)
Total Money Available		$ 8,530.00	$ 7,660.00	$ 6,790.00	$ 5,920.00	$ 5,050.00	$ 3,580.00	$ 2,710.00	$ 1,840.00	$ 970.00	$ 100.00

Planning out your entire spending habits months in advance can be challenging as many of us don't know our lives that far in advance but the principle is the same. Plan as far ahead as you can, I prefer to forecast money flow no more than one year out where each month I update the plan removing the previous month and adding a new month. It's most important that the next few months are the most accurate where the later months can be a more unknowns as you have some time to adjust as needed.

List the anticipated income

List all your income you plan to bring in. It is better to be more conservative and guess low with incoming money. Being conservative will give you flexibility if you don't get as many hours at work initially anticipated. If you do get the hours, great! If you work hourly, then list out the number of hours you plan on working each week or month and the rate per hour. Don't forget to adjust your income by reducing the taxes and other deductions taken out of your paycheck before you receive it. A good estimate is between 15-25% of your paycheck will be reduced for taxes and other deductions before you see it. The goal is to list the amount of money you anticipate coming into your account each month. The total amount of money you must spend each month should be what you put down in anticipated income.

Income in this example only means money

coming in and not only from a job. For students, this may also include family contributions or gift cards for birthdays. In the above example, I listed out "Student Loans" as during this time, student loans were a source of income for me. Anything is fair game here, but I would also warn against adding things like "winning the lottery" or "Stock trading gains" that are volatile in the short term. The goal was to make it through the next 8 months, not the next 80 years.

After all the income categories are added together, you see how much money you have each week or month. An interesting thing in my example is I had more money at the beginning of each semester and the total each month in-between the start of the semester was minimal. When I noticed this trend, I could immediately see the need to spend money cautiously at the beginning of the semester (when expenses are also high from tuition and books). The more cautious I was at the beginning of each semester allowed me to have additional money at the end of the semester. I never ran out because I could see my money flow throughout my entire journey to my goal.

List the anticipated expenses.

List all your expenses you plan to have throughout the week or month. First start with those expenses which are most important and must be paid each month. Some of these expenses will be a set amount each month, like rent, a car payment, or a cable bill. Some will be varied each month depending on usage like the gas bill or the electric bill. They are expenses that typically cannot be missed without a penalty. We discussed earlier in the Dam model, control over our budgets rely more heavily on controlling the expenses (outflow) rather than the income (inflow). The thought is we can more easily cut our spending than bring in more money. This principle is why my expenses are usually more detailed. I can plan my expenses and list everything that separates me from my earned money. Be conservative with expenses by making each one a little higher than you believe will provide some wiggle room if things don't work out exactly as planned. Second, we list the non-mandatory expenses, or our wants. These are the fun expenses. Everyone needs fun in their life, but in a budget, these are the first to get cut when tough times are experienced. When I first create my budget layout, I almost always run out of money because my non-mandatory expenses are too high. Don't panic! I begin to taper back how much money I will spend until I have a balanced budget which shows that I will not run out of money by the end.

Now you have a plan!

The key to any budget is to stick to the plan. You list out all expenses and that is all the money you must spend. For example. I show I can spend $10/ month on movies. $10 cannot buy many movies, so when I go to the store and see a movie I really want to see, but last week I already purchased a movie, I must have the courage to stop myself from making the purchase. A budget is worthless if not holding us into a purchase behavior. What is the point of the bowling bumpers if they don't keep the ball from going into the gutter? Breaking the rules of the budget are very easy, especially early on when our bank account shows plenty of money as it did when I was in school. I received a big student loan payment at the beginning of the semester. Plenty of money to enjoy a bunch of great events around town.

The pain of not following the budget is rarely felt in the beginning, but rather in the end when the money is gone. I would also suggest this type of budget is great for a short time due to the stressful nature of following every small purchase and ensuring you don't run out of cash. This example is a year of college where typically a student saves a large amount of money, then attends school for 8-10 months. This highly monitored budget would also be good if you have recently lost your job for one reason or another. You list all your money available, list all your monthly expenses, and then you will be able to see how long you can maintain certain lifestyles without an income.

Medium Monitored Budget

A Medium Monitored Budget maintains much of the same concepts as the Highly Monitored Budget with the key difference in the detail of expense tracking. In the example below, the budget is laid out with the income at the top and all the expense categories. Remember this report is an estimate of all expenses looking forward into the future so many of them are a guess and can be adjusted as you learn more about your expenses throughout the year. I like to see one year ahead knowing the further away from today that I look, the "fuzzier" the numbers can get. Nobody knows what will happen one year from now, but the good thing is looking out that far ahead, you can see times where your wallet will get a little thin or where you might be able to afford a trip with your family or to see an old friend. I use this type of budget when life becomes more stable. I know the patterns of my income and for the foreseeable future I don't anticipate large changes to my situation. Use this type of budget to put money away for a rainy day.

Budget Medium Monitored

$	10,000.00											
Starting Money Available	August	September	October	November	December	January	Feburary	March	April	May	June	July
Anticipated Income	$2,600.00	$2,600.00	$2,600.00	$2,600.00	$2,600.00	$2,600.00	$2,600.00	$2,600.00	$2,600.00	$2,600.00	$2,600.00	$2,600.00

Expenses

Category	August	September	October	November	December	January	Feburary	March	April	May	June	July
Gas	(65.00)	(65.00)	(65.00)	(65.00)	(65.00)	(65.00)	(65.00)	(65.00)	(65.00)	(65.00)	(65.00)	(65.00)
Rent	(900.00)	(900.00)	(900.00)	(900.00)	(900.00)	(900.00)	(900.00)	(900.00)	(900.00)	(900.00)	(900.00)	(900.00)
Car Payment	(187.00)	(187.00)	(187.00)	(187.00)	(187.00)	-	-	-	-	-	-	-
Cell Phone	(95.00)	(95.00)	(95.00)	(95.00)	(95.00)	(95.00)	(95.00)	(95.00)	(95.00)	(95.00)	(95.00)	(95.00)
Food	(450.00)	(450.00)	(450.00)	(450.00)	(450.00)	(450.00)	(450.00)	(450.00)	(450.00)	(450.00)	(450.00)	(450.00)
Student Loan Repaymenet	(250.00)	(250.00)	(250.00)	(250.00)	(250.00)	(250.00)	(250.00)	(250.00)	(250.00)	(250.00)	(250.00)	(250.00)
Credit Card interest	(35.00)	(35.00)	(35.00)	(35.00)	-	-	-	-	-	-	-	-
Car Insurance	(450.00)	-	-	-	-	-	(450.00)	-	-	-	-	-
Utilities	(75.00)	(75.00)	(75.00)	(75.00)	(75.00)	(75.00)	(75.00)	(75.00)	(75.00)	(75.00)	(75.00)	(75.00)
Diapers/Baby Formula	(200.00)	(200.00)	(200.00)	(200.00)	(200.00)	(200.00)	(200.00)	(200.00)	(200.00)	(200.00)	(200.00)	(200.00)
Date Night	(150.00)	(150.00)	(150.00)	(150.00)	(150.00)	(150.00)	(150.00)	(150.00)	(150.00)	(150.00)	(150.00)	(150.00)
New Clothes	(50.00)	(50.00)	(50.00)	(50.00)	(50.00)	(50.00)	(50.00)	(50.00)	(50.00)	(50.00)	(50.00)	(50.00)
Home Expenses/Repairs	(50.00)	(50.00)	(50.00)	(50.00)	(50.00)	(50.00)	(50.00)	(50.00)	(50.00)	(50.00)	(50.00)	(50.00)
Savings	(75.00)	(75.00)	(75.00)	(75.00)	(75.00)	(75.00)	(75.00)	(75.00)	(75.00)	(75.00)	(75.00)	(75.00)
Total Money Available	$ 9,568.00	$ 9,586.00	$ 9,604.00	$ 9,622.00	$ 9,675.00	$ 9,915.00	$ 9,705.00	$ 9,945.00	$10,185.00	$10,425.00	$10,665.00	$10,905.00

After I married my wife Lauren, we adopted this type of budget. I held a stable job, and we were living in a modest apartment. We knew approximately the amount of money coming in and the amount leaving each month. Using this budget, we were able to adjust our spending up and down to meet our savings goals. Speaking in terms of the "Dam model", we knew the amount of water coming into the reserve and adjusted the outflow to meet those needs downstream. In a short period of time, we began to see our loans paid off and our savings begin to rise. We did not need to track every purchase as we understood generally the amount coming in and the amount going out. Instead, we tracked the category of spending and adjusted each month in each category to reach our goals. The Medium Monitored Budget is the typical budget you can find online and should be adapted when needed. Bottom line, the budget is about knowing how much money is coming into your dam reserve and adjusting the water released downstream so that a balance is set between the water coming in and leaving while also meeting all the needs upstream and downstream. The Medium Monitored Budget allows your track your progress as can be seen in the Total Money Available Row at the bottom of the table. If we are in August, we can look out 12 months and see our savings going up and the total money available increasing telling us we are bringing more money in than spending. This is financial freedom and can lead to having additional money to invest and increasing your take home income.

Low Monitored Budget

I believe every person needs a budget. Wealthy or poor. Yes, I would even recommend the wealthiest people on the planet to have a budget. There should be no surprise being wealthy can provide some advantages to staying within a budget, however, what you define as wealthy might not be the same as the person next to you. The Low Monitored Budget, as presented below, is a high-level view of your finances and should be used when you have been living below your income a long time, know your income and expenses, and are no longer in a growth mentality, but in a financially stable situation.

Over a lifetime, people grow accustomed to a lifestyle. There are individuals who win the lottery or inherit riches yet refuse to change their daily routines. When you've stabilized your expenses to the point that your current lifestyle will not change enough to ever exceed your income, the low monitored budget is useful. The low monitored budget is still needed so you can have peace of mind knowing the flow of money as it enters and exits your wallet. Any successful business known for having large amounts of money still maintains a budget and tracks money in and money out. Not necessarily because they believe they will run out of money, but because they want to protect the investment they've earned. Like the successful business, upon reaching the point we can use the low monitored budget, we should do it to protect the hard work we've gone through to get to this point.

Low Monitored Budget

$ 60,000.00	August	September	October	November	December	January	Feburary	March	April	May	June	July
Starting Money Available	$6,000.00	$6,000.00	$6,000.00	$6,000.00	$6,000.00	$6,000.00	$6,000.00	$6,000.00	$6,000.00	$6,000.00	$6,000.00	$6,000.00
Anticipated Income	$6,000.00	$6,000.00	$6,000.00	$6,000.00	$6,000.00	$6,000.00	$6,000.00	$6,000.00	$6,000.00	$6,000.00	$6,000.00	$6,000.00

Expenses

Category	August	September	October	November	December	January	Feburary	March	April	May	June	July
Home	(2,000.00)	(2,000.00)	(2,000.00)	(2,000.00)	(2,000.00)	(2,000.00)	(2,000.00)	(2,000.00)	(2,000.00)	(2,000.00)	(2,000.00)	(2,000.00)
Work	(300.00)	(300.00)	(300.00)	(300.00)	(300.00)	(300.00)	(300.00)	(300.00)	(300.00)	(300.00)	(300.00)	(300.00)
Family	(500.00)	(500.00)	(500.00)	(500.00)	(500.00)	(500.00)	(500.00)	(500.00)	(500.00)	(500.00)	(500.00)	(500.00)
Local Entertainment	(300.00)	(300.00)	(300.00)	(300.00)	(300.00)	(300.00)	(300.00)	(300.00)	(300.00)	(300.00)	(300.00)	(300.00)
Savings	(1,000.00)	(1,000.00)	(1,000.00)	(1,000.00)	(1,000.00)	(1,000.00)	(1,000.00)	(1,000.00)	(1,000.00)	(1,000.00)	(1,000.00)	(1,000.00)
Stock Options	(600.00)	(600.00)	(600.00)	(600.00)	(600.00)	(600.00)	(600.00)	(600.00)	(600.00)	(600.00)	(600.00)	(600.00)
International Travel	(1,000.00)	(1,000.00)	(1,000.00)	(1,000.00)	(1,000.00)	(1,000.00)	(1,000.00)	(1,000.00)	(1,000.00)	(1,000.00)	(1,000.00)	(1,000.00)
Total Money Available	$60,300.00	$60,600.00	$60,900.00	$61,200.00	$61,500.00	$61,800.00	$62,100.00	$62,400.00	$62,700.00	$63,000.00	$63,300.00	$63,600.00

As can be noted in the Low monitored budget, categories become even less detailed. The idea of this is as you have worked through using the Highly Monitored budget and the Medium Monitored budget, you've gained experience understanding the incoming and outgoing of your home budgets enough to become instinctive about what you can purchase and what you should go without.

The backbone of these three monitored budgets is an ever increasing (high to low) attention to detail. The highly monitored budget gives more attention to detail because the penalty for running out of money is large when compared to our budget. We do NOT want to run out of money and pay additional fees to the bank and late payment penalties to bill collectors. The low monitored budget gives less attention to detail because the penalty for going over the budget is much less. Each of us will switch between various types of budgets in our life but we constantly need to be aware of our needs and the situation we are in now.

While you consider your current situation, I encourage you to ask yourself these few questions and reflect on the answers which are provided. Each answer corresponds with one of the three described budgets. After answering all the questions, consider where you would best fit and then begin creating your personal budget.

Question #1:   Do you find yourself stressing each month over finances, especially near the end of each month?

Answers:

- Yes, Every Month (High)
- Yes, but not every month (Medium)
- No, I'm good (Low)

Question #2: Is your income expected to change in the next 12 months?

Answers:

- Yes, a change is coming, and it may be challenging (High)
- No, I'm good (Medium)
- Yes, it's a better financial position (Low)

Question #3: Do you find that you run out of money often or more often that you would like?

Answers:

- Yes, and I need to figure out how to make it stop (High)
- Not much but there is a chance it could happen again (Medium)
- No, I never have this problem (low)

Question #4: Do you anticipate your income changing (especially declining) in the next few months?

Answers:

- Yes, and I am worried how I will survive for a while (High)
- Not too much, I feel my income is stable for now (medium)
- Not at all, I know my needs are met for the near future (low)

Question #5: Is your daily routine anticipated to change soon?

Answers:

- Yes, A big change impacting my finances (High)
- Maybe, but it won't impact my expenses or income (Medium)
- No, I not seeing any big changes in the future (Low)

Question 6: Am I trying to save enough money for a large upcoming purchase?

Answers:

- Yes, I am motivated to save for the large purchase (High)
- Maybe, but I don't know for sure yet (Medium)
- No, I don't see any big purchase in my future (Low)

Question 7: Is my family or immediate family members expected to see a change soon?

Answers:

- Yes, my children will need something expensive soon (College, or a car, or a wedding, etc.) (High)
- They will, but not for a long while (Medium)
- No, all my kids are gone and have kids of their own (Low)

Question 8: Do you have a good idea of your income and expenses each month?

<u>Answers</u>
- No, I pay the bills that arrive but don't have the overall numbers (High)
- Some but if something changed, I wouldn't notice (Medium)
- Absolutely. If any bills were off, I would notice (Low)

Question 9: How often do you change your living situation?

<u>Answers</u>
- I move about once per year or frequent enough I don't bother fully unpacking (High)
- Every few years, we are looking to move or change our living situation (Medium)
- I'm very stable and plan to be in the same location for some time (Low)

Question 10: How comfortable are you with creating and following a budget?

<u>Answers</u>
- I hate budgets and feel like they restrict my ability to live free. (High)
- I budget some but mostly when I have a large purchase in the future (Medium)
- I enjoy budgeting and seeing how a good budget can help achieve my goals (Low)

A budget is only as useful as the ability to follow them. Question 10 came about while speaking with a few people about their budgeting habits. I found if the person enjoys following a budget, their finances were most likely in a better condition, and they did not need a robust budget system. The opposite was also true. A person who needed financial help usually despised budgeting. When I asked why this happens, I saw those who hated budgeting, hated so because they felt trapped or limited while following a budget. The budget shined a light on bad spending behaviors and ultimately made the person feel worse about their financial situation. If done correctly, budgets should provide valuable and actionable insight into your spending habits. You take the information, make changes, and then begin to see a positive impact to savings. Those who enjoy budgeting have seen that happen repeatedly, leading to a wealthy and happy outlook on the process. Those who hate budgeting only see the challenge and hardship it caused them. If you make a budget, a I highly suggest you do, I recommend making actionable changes to your spending habits from the information in the budget. If not, you will only become frustrated and annoyed at the lack of progress.

Lessons Learned in Forecasting the Weather (Goals and Budgeting)

- Budgets are needed at every stage of life and vary for each person.
- High Monitored Budgets are very detailed and needed during times of change.
- Medium Monitored Budgets are less detailed and needed during times of stability and growth.
- Low Monitored Budgets are least detailed and needed during times of long-term stability and ease.
- Making a budget is worthless unless followed.
- Budgets can lead to happiness and financial growth, or they can lead to frustration and financial decline… they shine a light on your purchase habits, good or bad.
- You can change your spending habits by making good actionable changes found in a budget.

Notes

CHAPTER 12

THE CASH SYSTEM

"A budget tells us what we can't afford, but it doesn't
keep us from buying it."
~ William Feather

One of the hardest things to do is go from a period with
plenty of money and living under a certain budget to one
of reduced money earned each month. For me this
happened when I returned to graduate school after 8
years of working full time. Literally one day I was working
and the next day I had no job and had no plans to work
for the following 21 months! My family was about to go
down a very tough road financially and we needed to
make some severe changes to the way money was to be
spent. My wife and I talk a great deal about life decisions;
especially big decisions which impact the family and
entering graduate school was no different. We knew our
spending habits needed to change and most likely we
were going to switch from a medium monitored budget
to a more granular highly monitored budget. One big
topic of discussion was the challenge of changing our
habits. We both are very good at sticking to budgets but
changing habits can be tricky, so we developed a cash

system. We created a game between ourselves while at the same time almost forcing ourselves to stop purchases or face running out of money before our bank accounts would be depleted.

Credit cards are everywhere in society, and we are even transferring to a card-less system where you can pay with your watch or phone by swiping it over a device on the counter. This creates an action where we can easily forget how much money we spend each day and very easily lose track of $20 purchases made multiple times each day. We spoke to great detail about this in earlier chapter on Financial Abstraction. Knowing about financial abstraction, my family created a highly monitored budget. We tracked every dollar spent because we knew we had to plan or be in real financial trouble. Separating the mandatory purchases from the non-mandatory purchases, we devised a plan to use credit cards for the standard purchases made each month like rent, insurance, groceries, and other purchases which were regular and routine. This allowed us to gain cash back benefits on the cards we used to help with fun events later.

We then looked at the non-mandatory expenses and decided these can be controlled through a cash system. At the beginning of each month, we budget how much money we can each spend on things like going out to eat, movies, or other non-mandatory items. If any of us wanted to make a non-mandatory purchase, we had to ask ourselves, do we want it bad enough to spend our cash on it. To encourage this saving behavior, we made a little competition /game each month. Whoever had the most money saved at the end of the month earned a treat using the other person's cash. These treats were small in price and were usually a candy bar or soda, but the competition took much of the drudgery out of cutting back purchases. Making the hardship a game, it became fun to ask each other how much money we had remaining as the end of the month came near. This game continually increased the desire to spend less.

One word of caution though on the cash game. The main goal is to decrease spending and place more in savings. I've noticed a desire when working in cash is to cheat and there is ample ability to cheat a budget when spending with cash. You do the cash system because you need to make a change. If you cheat, you are only cheating yourself. Any money remaining at the end of each month should not be added to the next month new total. It should be put back into savings and you start over in the new month. If you have remaining money, it means you did it! If you don't have remaining money, it's ok. Pick yourself up, readjust and reset for the new month.

Most individuals become adapt to a certain lifestyle and cutting the lifestyle back can lead to difficulty in depression, marriage challenges, feeling of failure, and much more. I suggest if you are facing a significant decrease in income and need to cut expenses, begin by following the following list:

1.   Craft a new high monitored budget using your new earnings and all anticipated expenses.

2.   If you have a partner, plan out who is responsible for what expenses. It's important to be on the same page. If one person is responsible for a certain expense, they can consider ways (like coupons, or other savings) to reduce the expense as the expert in that category.

3.   Align your expenses, ensuring you can cover all expenses and remove non-mandatory expenses if needed. You may also need to cut back on mandatory expenses such as moving to a smaller home or selling a car. This is the Dam Model: Make sure there is a balance between the money coming in and going out.

4.   Estimate the available money which can be spent on non-mandatory items. These items are the fun stuff in your life that won't really hurt you if you stop doing them and take out this amount of money in cash each month. By doing this you remove financial abstraction and see the value you give when you receive a product or service.

5.   Anytime you want to purchase an item on the non-mandatory list, use cash. Doing this allows you to see how quickly purchases can separate you from your money. Hopefully, you see how quickly it can be

gone and you then are able to reduce spending and stick within the planned budget. Make a game out of it by setting tiers of prizes. If you have $5 remaining each month, you can buy a candy bar. If you have $10 remaining each month, you can buy yourself your special Starbucks drink. If you have $100 remaining, treat yourself to your favorite burger place with a friend. It's more about balance than about taking away the good things in life.

6.   See your habits change and begin saving while also staying within budget.

The cash system is challenging to maintain over long periods of time, but it can really assist with changing spending habits and staying within a budget. There are also ways to make it enjoyable. Use the cash system to control spending but also make it a little more fun to spend money. How often to you get to spend cash nowadays. Everything is on a debit or credit card.

Lessons Learned in The Cash System

- Use cash as a budget enforcer. You better see the impact of giving value to make a purchase.
- Take the sting out of reducing expenses by making a competition or reward out of it.
- The cash system lets you see how fast money can be spent.
- Don't Cheat! You only hurt yourself and your goals.
- If you don't succeed, pick yourself up, readjust and reset for the next month!
- You Got THIS!

Notes

CHAPTER 13

CHANGE THROUGH LIFE AND THE TRANSITONS

"Just when I think I have learned the way to live, life changes."

~ Hugh Prather

Life inherently changes. We learn, we grow, and we change. Our finances will do the same. According to the Economic News Release by the US Bureau of Labor Statistics in September 2018, the average waged or salaried employee will stay in that job only 4.6 years before changing to a different role or a different company. Younger employees change jobs more frequently at 3.2 years on average. Because of these changes our finances will also change. Learning to control our spending habits will help ensure the transitions happen smoothly. Moving jobs and companies is always a challenging time. Taking the worry away from our financials will help getting up to speed in the new role and help find the balance between work and life.

If you consider a traditional career path, statistically a person right out of college earns the lowest wages they will ever earn in their entire career. This makes sense as they are new. They are new to the work force and unvetted and therefore risky and untrained in a professional career. Over the course of a few years, they become proven, experienced, and less risky so they earn more money. Usually, in the beginning of our careers we are very driven and work late nights to prove our increased value. This continues to happen until a certain point in our lives and then our priorities might change, and we begin to work less and less until we fully retire. When we retire our paychecks become smaller. We can think of this as a hill or a rollercoaster where in the beginning we start at the bottom of the hill, make it to the top, and then come down the other side. Hopefully we have saved enough money through the good years of income, we can now live off the savings. As good of a model as this is, it is no surprise it's not perfect, and we can see many times where the rollercoaster might look very different due to changes occurred throughout our life. It might look like this with multiple ups and downs.

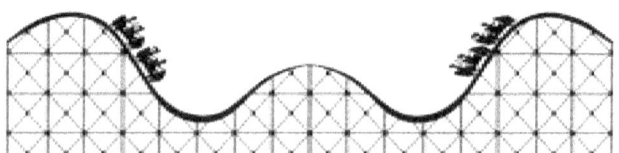

Or even crazier with loops and turns along the way.

As we have mentioned before, the key to manage the downturns is to manage your expenses. Life will determine your income at times because of job loss, or unexpected illness, or any unplanned event in life, but you can always control your expenses. No matter where you are on your crazy life rollercoaster, to live in financial freedom, make sure your expenses are less than your income.

In 2013, I was working in New Mexico and was recently married. I had just gone through a big adjustment of transitioning from a single life with a good income to a married life and now supporting a spouse who was still in her final year of undergraduate education at a local university. Within a few months my life would change again when I would accept a new job in Washington, D.C. In March 2014, my family and I packed our life and moved across the country to begin a new journey in the capital of the United States. The large challenge ahead was I was earning the exact same salary in Washington as

I was earning in Albuquerque, New Mexico. The problem… D.C. is more than twice the price of living. Our apartment in New Mexico was $800 per month and I lived 5 minutes from work in rush hour and 15 minutes to the downtown area. In Washington D.C., our rent was $1500 per month, and I lived almost 2 hours from work each way. The job was exciting, and I wanted a new adventure, so we were happy for the change, but our budget had to change dramatically. Eating at home was more of a priority and looking for ways to cut back became a needed exercise each month. We went as a family from the medium monitored budget in Albuquerque to a highly monitored budget in D.C. Though it was very difficult, we made it work and were even able to save some money which helped us move across the country a little over a year later to be closer to family.

Transitions frustrate plans whether the transition is planned or unplanned. There can be good in movement. Adding a child to your family can be a highlight of a lifetime while also adding stress and financial worry to caregivers. Ensuring the financial freedom of everyone under the budget is the goal and the better you can prepare for the changes, the better prepared you will be to change your spending habits as needed.

The image of a beach city preparing for a hurricane is one that comes to mind when I hear of families going through a difficult time financially. With weather technology today, we often hear of impeding storms days, if not weeks, in advance. This warning allows homeowners and business owners time to board up the windows, fill sandbags and place them strategically around the front door. If given enough time, damage can be limited, and life can resume almost immediately following the storm. This is a tremendous use of technology! Preparation reduces damage and saves lives! The same is with managing the transitional storms of life. If we are prepared, we can avoid damage and set us up in a way to resume a normal life once the storm has passed. What in your life can you see as a major in-coming change? By preparing now, how can you set yourself up for success throughout and immediately after the storm?

Unfortunately, the opposite is also true. Imagine a beachfront homeowner who does not watch the news about an incoming storm. When the rain starts falling and the tide starts to rise, the homeowner scrambles to find boards for the windows and tries with all their might to fill sandbags before the water rushes in the front door. They not only have to do all the work as everyone else, but now do it in the pouring rain and howling wind. All things which slow progress and ultimately not done as well as others. That homeowner will have more damage to fix after the storm. So as with our management of life transitions, if we do not see the financial storm coming, management of the storm becomes frantic and damaging.

There are many actions in life which happen to us that we cannot foresee. Job loss and death can happen suddenly. Even so, we can set aside a safety fund to help in those times of need. A little safety net provides a restful sleep when everything else around us is raging. Even the beach homeowner can have bags of sand prefilled or pre-purchased wood shutters for his windows avoiding the last-minute run to the store to find materials. What can you do today in preparation for unforeseen transitions in life?

The last item I will talk about in transitions is the unrealistic expectation we have to predict all of life's challenges. The unpredictability in life is what gives it the fun factor or the sparkle of waking up and being engaged in life. No two days are the same and we would drive ourselves mad planning for every possibility which could happen to us. Not to mention spend WAY too much money on things which would never happen. Look at your life and the life of your close friends and family. It would be a good bet; you will encounter similar transitions in life as they once did. Ask them how they survived and what they would do differently if they could.

As I've asked people what's their "secret sauce" to living well, one common theme has always been the lesson of sacrificing early and the benefits those sacrifices brought down the road. This is extremely true in finances. A little sacrifice early pays large dividends later in life when we shoulder more responsibility for larger families, co-workers, and larger life expectations.

Lessons Learned in Change in Life and Transitions

- Change is inevitable. Prepare for it and you will avoid unnecessary last-minute spending.
- We will all go through up and downs with income. We can only control the expenses.
- Being prepared brings stability and ease in trying times.

Notes

CHAPTER 14

WEALTH AND WHAT IT MEANS

"There is a gigantic difference between earning a great deal of money and being rich."
~ Marlene Dietrich

In August 2016, I entered a full-time MBA program. My motivation for taking two years off work was to have hopes of breaking through a management ceiling I had noticed more and more during my previous years of work experience. I thought, if I were to make more money, I would enjoy my job more because I would have the money to enjoy my life. I do believe this statement to be somewhat true. There is a good country song that says, "money can't buy happiness, but it can buy me a boat".. Whenever I hear that on the radio, I sing it loud and proud! During my first year of graduate school, I gained a good friend in my program who opened my eyes to the term "wealth". I spent that first year really considering the term and what it meant for me and my family.

I have mentioned a few times in this book the term "financial freedom". The two terms of being wealthy and being financially free are different but connected. Gaining financial freedom is the first step to becoming wealthy. Becoming financially free means living within your means. Being wealthy is the perspective of the person and often includes much more than just a healthy savings account. Balance between work and play, money in and money out, or income and expenses. You cannot obtain the balance needed to feel wealthy without first having obtained financial freedom.

Wealth has a different meaning to anyone you ask and there are certainly more definitions than provided by me. The greatest lesson learned on the meaning of wealth came when I met a man names Joseles in Salt Lake City. Joseles was the happiest man I've ever met. He knew is priorities in life and he genuinely cared about everyone he met. He spoke very limited English and most people at work called him "Abuelo" meaning "grandfather" in Spanish due to his elderly age and his caring demeanor. He was one of the humblest men both morally and financially I've ever known. For a greater part of his life, Joseles was a janitor and had a large family. For many years, Joseles walked a few miles to work each way until, in his later years, he joined a carpool. He arrived each afternoon and working into the evening. Upon arriving at work, he would gingerly work around the office space asking others about their children and work demands. Always smiling and always cheerful he brought happiness to the office. It was not long after I knew him, that Joseles began to struggle and have severe stomach pain. Doctors found pancreatic cancer and within a few short months, he passed into the next life. While attending his funeral, I realized how "wealthy" Joseles really was in life. A simple man with little need for material possessions, the meeting house was packed. Individuals from multiple states had come to give final goodbyes to a man who touched their life. He was a janitor. Many would not see this act as life changing or able to make a difference in the lives of others, but Joseles created daily wealth. Joseles used his small time passing the office to talk to you and make you feel loved. He lived within his means and generated wealth unlike I've ever seen.

Wealthy to you can mean dollars in your pocket or time with loved ones. Just asking around your circle of influence will create several different answers. One consistency found to being wealthy is having the ability to move and act as one desires. To spend time with family instead of being tied to a desk or to take the annual vacation instead of staying home. To accomplish the goal of becoming "wealthy" in your eyes, the first step is to gain control of your finances and ensure you are living within your means. Gain financial freedom. You cannot become free to pursue your passions if you are tied to others through debt or other financial burdens.

So many resources are available promising to increase your riches and provide more money. Some are real and some are fake but learning to control your expenses is most often the easiest and most ignored way to increase your wealth. Watching your small spending habits creates large savings and ability to be financially free.

Death by $20 shares a simple idea where people can lose everything over habitually spending $20 multiple times per day. Seeing more money leave than come in destroys wealth and freedom. I like to think money does not buy happiness, but being financial captive causes stress, anxiety, additional debt, and additional problems. Those are not any part of my happiness. All avoidable and preventable problems. Gain financial freedom by removing the unnecessary items in your life, reduce your spending and live within your means.

Lessons Learned in Wealth and What it Means.

- Having lots of money does not mean you are wealthy.
- You must first be financially free to become wealthy.

Notes

ABOUT THE AUTHOR

JR is a guy trying to understand why so many struggle with finances and give insight into ways to help. Since an early age, he was a saver. It came naturally. I loved seeing my bank statement as a 10-year-old and seeing the numbers grow. I would pass on treats or the latest gaming system because I was saving money as a 16-year-old. He did everything from mowing lawns, to working odd jobs to put away as much as he could at an early age. Even putting money from birthdays and Christmas into the bank. Russ's passion to understand everyday financial struggles came when he would meet those who on paper seem to have plenty of funds, but often are left penniless each month. Reviewing their financials, he came to see that most don't go bankrupt because of large homes or overpriced cars, but it's the small purchases that add up each day. $20 here and $20 there.

JR sees great need for simple, straight-forward teachings on the basics of money instead of the 1000's of "do this and get rich overnight" books. As a teen he caught a bug of saving which has helped him overcome many financial hardships in life. He wants this mindset to be the base that others can build wealth creation from instead of the other way around. Reading only the get rich quick books give people more anxiety than help. They are great to pump up an ego or bring excitement, but that excitement won't last longer than the next credit card statement if expenses are not kept in check.

While he has worked in many corporate and government positions building scalable processes and programs, he came to realize the everyday person is at a disadvantage from the start. These companies have war rooms discussing how to separate you from your money. They want more and that means you have less. His goal with this book is to bring to light some of the tactics companies use in the marketing game as well as provide a feeling of empowerment as you approach budgeting and spending. Money is a complex concept and we all could use a refresher to what it represents in our life.

Bibliography

ii   https://content.schwab.com/web/retail/public/about-schwab/Charles-Schwab-2019-Modern-Wealth-Survey-findings-0519-9JBP.pdf?_ga=2.178023200.448759496.1597951586-566447588.1597951586

ii   https://www.waterstonegroup.com/insights-and-news/americas-relationship-with-subscription-services/

iii   https://www.marketwatch.com/story/youre-spending-more-on-your-subscription-services-than-you-think-2018-07-25

iv   https://www.census.gov/library/stories/2019/09/us-median-household-income-not-significantly-different-from-2017.html

vvvv   https://content.schwab.com/web/retail/public/about-schwab/Charles-Schwab-2019-Modern-Wealth-Survey-findings-0519-9JBP.pdf?_ga=2.178023200.448759496.1597951586-566447588.1597951586

vi   https://www.nerdwallet.com/blog/average-credit-card-debt-household/

vii   (*https://www.cbsnews.com/news/cutting-through-advertising-clutter/),

viii   https://www.federalreserve.gov/paymentsystems/2017-December-The-Federal-Reserve-Payments-Study.htm

www.ingramcontent.com/pod-product-compliance
Lightning Source LLC
Chambersburg PA
CBHW070556220526
45467CB00003B/1222